Alive & Well

Alive & Well

Awakening to Your Angels

Ashley George

©2025 All Rights Reserved. No portion of this book may be reproduced, stored in a retrieval system, or transmitted in any form or by any means—electronic, mechanical, photocopy, recording, scanning, or other—except for brief quotations in critical reviews or articles without the prior permission of the author.

Published by Game Changer Publishing

Cover Design: Skylar Cawley

Paperback ISBN: 978-1-966659-61-7

Hardcover ISBN: 978-1-966659-62-4

Digital ISBN: 978-1-966659-63-1

www.GameChangerPublishing.com

Dedication

To my Adelyn, you were the one who sparked so much change in me the second I saw you. I felt overcome with purpose in such a deep way. I will forever be grateful. The light you are in this world is nothing short of magical. Your kindness, creativity, and gentleness will only add value to others' lives if they are lucky enough to know you. Because you only make things better. Always stay true to who you really are; never change for others. Thank you for choosing me to be your mom; I love you forever and always.

To my Tripp, having a son has opened my eyes and heart to so much that I didn't have before. I'm forever grateful for this. Your competitive spirit, your humor, and your curiosity make you uniquely you. Never stop seeing the world with your wondrous and curious heart. Never stop asking questions and seeking answers. I know you have big dreams, and I believe they are placed in your heart for a reason. Never give up! Thank you for choosing me as your mom. I love you forever and always.

To my Lilah, you will always be my favorite birthday gift. Being around you is seeing life with pure JOY and magic. I pray this always stays in your heart. Never let the world change this about you. It's too special. I know you can feel deeply as well, and this will only provide pure empathy for all those around you. Shine your light bright always; never dim it to make others feel comfortable because I think your very bright light will change the world someday. Thank you for choosing me as your mom. I love you forever and always.

To Alan, I'm so grateful for you allowing me to 100% be me the last few years. You never doubted me. You never made me feel as if I were crazy. You were only proud, curious, and supportive. This support gave me the courage to keep going even when I was so fearful of what others may think and was so close to giving up so many times. It continued to push me down this path and to help bring this book out there for the world to read. Thank you for everything you do for our family. You are truly loved and so appreciated.

Read This First

Just to say thanks for buying and reading my book, I would like to give you a free gift—*Connect to the most authentic version of yourself: A guide to connecting with the Archangels,* no strings attached!

Scan the QR Code to Download:

Alive & Well

AWAKENING TO YOUR ANGELS

ASHLEY GEORGE

Contents

	Read This First	1
	Introduction	7
1.	Awakening	13
2.	Mind, Body, and Spirit	25
3.	Religion	33
4.	Our Souls	41
5.	Our Human Life; Let's Help Each Other Be Human	51
6.	Old Souls	59
7.	Heaven-Like	65
8.	Is There Such a Thing as Bad Souls?	71
9.	Spiritual Gifts	85
10.	Angels	95
11.	My First Angel Connection: Archangel Gabriel	103
12.	Archangel Michael	117
13.	Archangel Raphael	123
14.	Archangel Jophiel	127
	Conclusion	131
	Thank You for Reading my Book!	135

Introduction

In today's world/society, there is so much noise that comes from all different directions. It's so hard to break free at times from the heaviness of this noise and allow ourselves to live with our true spirit—the spirit that we were born and created to be—leading the way. I really want this book to be an inspiration for you, no matter what chapter you are currently living in or your life circumstances. I want this to inspire you to silence the noise and break free to live your most authentic self with your light shining so very brightly. I want you to truly listen to that voice from within, start to get to know your true self, and be brave enough to listen. What do you really need to do to set yourself on the path to finding your truest self—the path you planned for yourself before coming into this world? The one that you and God truly wanted for your soul in this lifetime? What do you think that is? Do you feel like you are currently on that path? How can we tell? These are all the amazing questions that I hope you start to ask yourself. What is truly your bigger purpose in this lifetime? And how do you start living it?

Life is not about being perfect or finding that perfect path. It's truly not possible. We are human, after all, but it should feel good to be alive. It should feel as though you are in a flow that brings magic to you every day, excitement, joy, and presence. It should feel good to think about the future and what is truly possible. There really is so much magic in our everyday patterns, but we have to be open to seeing this. It's hard to do this for many reasons throughout our lives. I completely understand this myself. I feel like I had lost the *magic* feeling of life and became a robot, in a sense. I was surviving to get through the day instead of thriving and allowing my family to thrive as well. I felt disconnected from myself, and I couldn't understand why. I felt like I was completing all the steps to live a healthy lifestyle, so why didn't I feel healthy? I was tired all the time, not joyful about the little things, and had zero motivation. I didn't feel like myself, I wasn't creative, and I was desperate for an answer.

I went to my doctor to get every lab possible. I had believed in root cause medicine—a lot of times called functional medicine—for so long that I felt like I was already doing everything I needed to live life in optimal health. We went through all the testing. I was sure we would find something and I could fix this issue. When we found nothing, I felt even more discouraged. I thought I would have my answer to my problems and I would be on my way. I didn't know what to do anymore. I was doing all the things the outside noise was telling me to do, working out, eating healthy, sleeping, I mean everything to "be healthy." I hated feeling this way. And why had all this been working for me years prior, but all of a sudden, it all seemed to come to a screeching halt? I will tell you I was desperate to find the answers. My doctor had even suggested depression medication because my symptoms absolutely sounded like I was describing this. I completely understand it sounds like that! I was so desperate; I was willing to try anything! I tried them for maybe a week and did not like the feeling. I trusted this was not the path for me. I felt even more tired on the medication, and I just knew deep down there had to be another way. I know medication can be lifesaving at times for some people, but I think I knew the problem was something way deeper for me and would not be solved by covering it up with medication. I wanted to get to the root of this.

I continued to feel like I needed to do something to fix myself. I became incredibly guilty because I hated that I couldn't always feel like myself for my kids or family. I was just *so* tired. I could barely get through the day. This came with a lot of shame/guilt/lack of worthiness. Did anyone know this on the outside? Absolutely not.

I kept praying for answers. I also was asking myself what would help me: *Am I doing something that isn't what I want to do anymore? What would that be? I have a beautiful life. I should just feel lucky and grateful and go about my day. I have a healthy and beautiful family. Shame on me for not feeling or questioning if this is all I want. I can think about that sometime later, right? Down the road. Not now! I just need to be grateful and show up for my family in many different ways!*

Well, have you heard of burnout? I had. But was there such a thing as motherhood burnout? I had never heard anyone really talk about this. How can we actually be burned out from the very things that our heart loves the most and the people who are such a gift to us that we would give our lives for? It could not be possible that I was just experiencing burnout of life in general, could it?

I feel like the burnout of motherhood was truly getting to me. But honestly, it wasn't just motherhood; it was all the noise piling on top of me. I just didn't know this at the time. This is hard and scary for me to even write down that motherhood was burning me out. That was my job! I was the main caregiver to my children. I was even more mad at myself because we had a beautiful life. Why couldn't I feel like myself? I got to be home with my kids, had a beautiful home, and everything we needed, so why couldn't I just be excited about this? Why couldn't I feel joyful and present? Let's rewind a few years prior when I didn't feel this way. I loved all the small moments, days, and all the things. I felt great! I couldn't understand where this was all getting tangled and going wrong. What happened that made me start to enjoy these things less?

I don't know about you guys, but there is a lot of pressure on parents these days. *A lot.* Also, when you live with zero family to help you, are anxiety-ridden about babysitters, and have a husband with a high-pressure and powerful job who travels often, let me tell you, this can all start to feel a bit heavy. This is where that noise comes back into our lives. The noise urging us to check the 600 emails from school (okay,

I'm exaggerating, but you get the idea!), activities, sign-up forms, articles about what to do and what not to do with your kids, playdates, lessons, schoolwork, nutrition, the "do's and don'ts" of everything, whether to homeschool your children or not—it's overwhelming. It never ends. I mean, we can go on and on and on. I really started to feel overwhelmed by all the outside noise. Constantly. I felt a lot of pressure coming from every direction. And it was not just motherhood outside noise; it was noise about life in general.

I understand now, from this perspective, what was happening. I was letting all the noise come into my energetic field. I was literally *feeling* the noise. I was building more and more heaviness, anxiety, and less joy each day. I was allowing all the outside noise of the world to pile high on top of me and my heart. I just didn't realize this was what I was doing and the situation I was creating for myself. I thought I was being a good mom. I thought I *had* to do all the things the noise from the outside was telling me to do to feel good about myself. If I did those things, I would be the perfect mom. I would feel great myself. I would have the perfect kids that would grow up with zero trauma, be so happy, so successful, and love life. I thought if I listened to all the outside noise, I would have the answers to raise my kids in such a blissful way, and they would be on their path to greatness even if their mom was deeply suffering to get them there.

I felt as though the noise had piled so high that the heaviness ultimately led me to quite a different and unexpected path—a miracle in a sense. I realized I had to quiet the noise, calm the anxiety, and eliminate the negative thoughts. The noise "bubble" that I felt as though I was drowning in had to be shattered, I couldn't take it anymore. I had to find my peace, which was nowhere to be found outside of me. I had to understand it was all within me. Other people's voices, opinions, and paths were not my own. This was not easy and didn't happen overnight for me, but I want to share with you my true awakening.

If you had asked me even just a few years ago what a spiritual awakening was, I would have had zero clue what you were talking about. If you had told me I would be writing a book about how to return to our soul selves, how to connect with the angels, God, and all those things, I would have thought you were *crazy*. So, if you are thinking this yourself right now, that is absolutely okay. I want to share my own story, teach what I now know, and help others who may be asking themselves all these same questions. I want to help others who also may be feeling the heaviness of the noise. I welcome every person from different religious backgrounds, life circumstances, genders, and races to read my book. Because you will learn that I deeply believe we are all connected. You ALL matter.

If you are reading this book, I promise you were led to these exact words for a reason. Let me tell you, friends, there is so much magic in our everyday life, and I want to teach you how to find it. I want to teach you how to quiet the noise and start listening to your own soul's voice. Your own path. And not just your own soul's voice, but the voices of the angels as well and the divine wisdom that is all around you every day. It is trying to help us every step of the way with everything life throws at us. From the smallest things to the biggest hurdles, they are here to help us. We just forget they are there, or we don't believe in them at all.

Your journey and path may look different from everyone else's or even mine, and that is okay. We all have our own path to our awakenings. How do we become brave enough to listen to what is calling out for us to follow and get us on the right path? I am sending so much encouragement to you as you read this. I know you can do it because we all came here to do so. This doesn't mean you will leave your family or your job to pick up and move across the world tomorrow. No! It means you will start to listen to the voice telling you how to get to the places that your soul wants you to get to. Maybe that eventually is a change in careers, more travel, asking for more help, starting a business, finding love, or whatever your highest path is. Or maybe it's connecting to the simplicity of life in general. Being more present in the life you already live. Living life with more joy and gratitude. But this is all about how we can live our lives in such a way that we have love, compassion, and worthiness for ourselves and for each other! We must learn to trust ourselves again and truly step into our own power and our connection with our divine self. Once we start to feel that connection from within our own hearts, raise our vibrations, and feel connected, we are helping humanity as a whole. We are connected to a higher consciousness. It's a ripple effect that will travel to all those around you. I think we all need this now more than ever before.

CHAPTER 1

Awakening

"The day of my spiritual awakening was the day I saw and knew I saw all things in God and God in all things."
– Mechtild of Magdeburg

What is truly a spiritual awakening? Well, I googled it, and here are a few answers I got. This is from Google, AI review definition: A personal transformation that involves a shift in worldview and mental framework and a call to a deeper level of consciousness. It can be a profound experience that many people go through, but it may not always be talked about. Some signs of a spiritual awakening can include heightened intuition, increased empathy and sensitivity, more vivid dreams, feeling a deep connection with the universe, a desire to be honest with yourself, a sense of unity with all, and changes in beliefs wanting to serve others.

So, what in the world does that mean? Well, I will share a little about my own awakening, what I think it really means, and how others can experience their own awakening journeys. To me, that's all I really think it is: a journey back to remembering your true self.

My awakening happened in many ways, with attempts to break me free throughout the years—perhaps with little nudges here and there since childhood—but my first major breakthrough came when I became a mom. I now look back and can almost feel that shift. I instantly felt overcome with purpose. This also shifted into a deep and powerful path that placed me on the wellness path. I remember feeling strongly: *I have to take care of myself so I can be strong not only physically but mentally and emotionally for my daughter.* Even though I grew up participating in sports and playing volleyball, even in college, I never was super into wellness or health. It's like a part of me started waking up to pay attention to it as I knew I needed to. And I promise you, it will all connect later down the road. It was my first big push or nudge, and I listened.

Over the next eight or so years, I really listened to that voice. I jumped deep into the wellness industry. I became incredibly knowledgeable about the ingredients of food, toxins in products, physical strength, and so much more. I started a small lifestyle blog and went to town trying to inspire others in hopes of also creating a shift inside of them. I wrote about paying attention to what's going into our body, how important movement is, and how this is actually all connected to motherhood as well—the wholeness aspect. If we take care of ourselves, we can take care of others, correct? I felt so passionate about this, about lifting not only myself up but other women and helping them feel the same about themselves. This is also what I loved about my job as a hairstylist for ten years in downtown Chicago before becoming a mom. I love to make people feel good about themselves while being creative. I always have. That's why I turned to blogging after becoming a mom. Moving from Chicago to Charlotte, not knowing anyone, and being a stay-at-home mom for the first time was a lot at first. But also I loved it. I really did. I loved experiencing the new city, I loved spending time with my daughter, and I got to know myself a little better as well.

After about a year of being home with my daughter and being pregnant with my son, I knew I started to miss having a creative outlet. I needed to connect to other women and use my creative energy. This is when my little lifestyle blog entered the world. It was a perfect fit at first. I used my creative energy to put together outfit inspirations for other moms, recipes that made me feel good, kid recipes, and so on. It was an outlet for me. I could talk about all my new health and wellness knowledge. And my passion for it. It's as if my heart and soul knew I wanted to talk about things I'm passionate about, but I covered it up with light-hearted posts about styled outfits. Ha, it sounds a bit ridiculous. I had photo captions, maybe as long as this book at times, because my heart had a lot to say.

But I now understand what was happening. It was a little puzzle piece that I took a chance on and was being nudged to explore. I needed those skills. I needed to know how to build a platform, work with other companies, and find like-minded communities. It was a lot of fun. I learned a lot, and I'm really proud of myself for taking a chance on it. Not everyone understood what I was doing at the time, so it was also a time I had to push through some noise and stay true to what I wanted to do. I also learned I needed that little space on the web because I truly needed to have a place where my creative energy could share what I was passionate about. It allowed me to shift and grow along with it.

I'm not here advocating for social media in any way, shape or form. I think there are positives for adults like myself who want to connect and be inspired by others, make money, and grow a like-minded community. But I also think there are a lot of negatives. It's important to remember that YOU are in control of yourself, what you watch, or who you follow. It's all your choice! What makes you feel good, and what does not? And maybe none of it makes you feel good; it's not your thing. That is completely okay! We are all different. Our heart and soul speaks to us all differently. You get to decide what noise you are letting in. No one else has control over that besides yourself. Also, let's remember we are adults; children do not have the brain development to understand this like we do. I don't think social media is a great choice for kids!

No matter what, I am personally very grateful I listened to that voice or that big shift that I felt after becoming a mom. I really dove into health and wellness and everything related to physical, emotional, and mental health. I would read books, take classes, listen, and read blogs. I loved learning everything I could that I felt aligned with. It made me happy, and I felt alive when I felt like I kept finding the truth. My passions grew, my website grew, and then I had a friend throw me a curveball and lead me to a different experience!

This is when I entered a pageant—yes, you heard me! Regardless of your beliefs about pageants, stay with me for a moment. Looking back now, I can see it was all part of a bigger plan, though I didn't understand it at the time. I often questioned myself, wondering if I was doing the right thing. Once again, I found myself asking what I had gotten into. Like so many times before, I laughed it off in the moment, but I'm glad I listened and pushed through the noise once again. I learned a lot from the people around me during that time. It didn't make sense back then, but now it does. I had already delved deep into physical health and emotional health, but this experience truly opened my eyes to the power of mental health. Our thoughts have the incredible ability to shape our emotional experiences and even influence physical outcomes and realities.

I will always be thankful that I was placed on that path. I met Heather, who taught me so much about mental management. She is a mental management coach who grew up with a father teaching this to Olympians all over the world. I had no idea that even existed before signing up for all this. I thought we would practice some interview questions and be on our way. I had no idea that she would impact me on a big level. I'm bringing this up to remind us all that sometimes, the path may not make sense at the time. Putting ourselves out there and trying different life experiences that may seem so silly to other people can be placed in front of us for a bigger reason. It may be because, on that path, you may meet one person that God has sent for you. It may be one tiny book, speech, a new friendship, or a situation that was meant to stay with you for the continued path created by your higher self. So, pay attention to the new experiences or people who ask you to try something different that is out of your comfort zone. Don't *not* do things because you are afraid of what others may think. Experience life! Take a chance!

I'm always thankful for what may seem so silly about that year to others. I signed up for that right before the world was completely shutting down, thanks to COVID-19. I had no idea what was coming into play with all this. As I signed the paperwork, I thought, *Well, this will give me a great goal to work on for a couple of months, then it will be done! I can push myself, have a goal for myself (which I like), and no one has to know. I've just had three kids in the past five years, so it will be fun to do something different! It will just be my little thing—for me.*

Well, that was great, but the pageant was supposed to take place in March 2020. We all know what March 2020 looked like, and our pageant kept getting pushed back, and back, and back, along with everything and everyone else's plans in the world. What I thought was going to be a short little fun goal for myself turned into ten months of hard work during COVID! I thought, *Of all the times to be doing hard work on ourselves, are you kidding me, God?* Our worlds were getting flipped upside down, and I had three small kids, all ages five and under. It was crazy, just like it was for everyone else. But I do feel like I had something different. I also had all that work I was already doing from the pageant goals. I had a physical, mental, and emotional coach built into my little system at home. I was physically focused at home and had a great trainer, Heather, on Zoom, who was helping me mentally and emotionally. If I hadn't signed up for that silly goal just weeks before COVID, I am not sure what that time would have looked like for me, to be honest. I'll never know. I will just be thankful and know that God sent that on my path for a reason.

I also won the pageant and became Mrs. North Carolina! Then I realized, oh shoot, now I have to tell people (*haha*)! That fear of what others may think and the outside noise of others came circling back in. But I once again pushed through.

I felt passionate about using my new platform, and I created a documentary all about the struggles mothers went through during that time mentally, physically, and emotionally. It was all because I took a chance that I felt like was being presented for a reason. I was meant to experience and learn things from all the people on my path in that short time. I can see it all like puzzle pieces now. It was one of the pieces I needed to find. I needed to go through that experience. It was part of my bigger plan, and it instilled knowledge within me of what our brains and thoughts are truly capable of. I will always be thankful to have learned how impactful one's mindset can be and how a deep understanding of this connection can be life-changing. It is not just some "woo-woo" sprinkled into positive thinking. True mindset and work on the mind can create new realities. I've lived and learned it. It will always stick with me. I'm forever grateful.

After that year, I slowed down a bit on my projects and my online business. Motherhood was always my first job; everything else always came when I could find time to fit something else in here or there. This is where I really started to question a lot, and I finally came to a screeching halt. I knew I felt a bit stuck. I was not sure what path I was supposed to be going down or where to turn to. I told myself daily I should probably just give this all up.

I knew I was passionate about mental, emotional, and physical health. I also knew how much everyone needed this—especially moms, and, honestly, parents in general. Everyone needs this! I was becoming frustrated, why wouldn't the universe just show up in the ways I wanted it to?! I was so passionate about everything I was talking about on my blog, podcast, and documentary. I cared deeply. I wanted everyone to know they could feel their best. I wanted the world to see, "Hey, look over here, my heart is really in this! I promise! I know this can help you!" But there was something missing. I could feel it. I always had, but I wanted to ignore it. I just wanted the universe to listen! I had put so much time and effort into all this stuff, and it was dramatically life-changing! It could help the whole world! The universe said, *"Ya, ya, ya, calm down, Ashley. You aren't supposed to get it quite yet."*

I never felt clear at that time about what in the world I was supposed to be doing with a little platform. I kept thinking, *God, just tell me what business I'm supposed to start with all of this—if any at all.* I was questioning all the things I'd learned. All the roads I had gone down. I felt as though I wasn't only missing something, but I wondered if I had anything to provide to people at all. Should I just give up? I was going in circles again... the complete opposite of mental management; let me remind you all. Here is proof that we need to take a few steps backward to move forward at different points in our lives. We are human, after all.

This is also where my real lack of creativity came in—my fatigue and frustration with wellness in general. This was all great until it wasn't for me anymore. Or so I started to think. I came to a screeching halt on my wellness journey and could not figure out what was going on. I became angry at wellness. It all became a bit too much for me. The voices screamed, *"Do this, eat this, don't eat that. Do this, and you will feel your best; do that, and you will feel better."* Advice started pouring in from all directions, and the noise piled up higher and higher—so much noise, so many opinions, as wellness became trendier and trendier. Eventually, I felt like I had turned my back completely on wellness. I thought, *None of this matters anymore. I don't feel good mentally, emotionally, and even physically anymore. People are too obsessed with all this, and it's no longer working for me personally.* This deeply upset me, even if I kept it all in. How could all of that been working for me, and now it's just not? I was so frustrated!

I also had no desire to create blog posts or inspiring content for others anymore. How could I? I myself didn't feel great or inspired. How could I possibly inspire others? I felt so stuck reading "woo-woo" books or content and rolled my eyes at the advice telling me to think more positively to change my life. I wanted to scream back, "Are you kidding?!" If only it were that easy. I think this was when I started to add in more wine for my personal diagnosis of "lost the magic of life." It was the only thing that would actually give me energy. It made me feel a bit like myself again and gave me some feeling at all. It helped calm the anxiety, or so I thought. I am not proud of that nor was it the answer I was looking for at all. It was a band-aid to the root issue. Like I know it is for so many others. The one thing I give myself credit for in this time was I continued to know there was an answer somewhere I was missing, and I trusted I would find it.

I also want to point out that I don't think anyone knew I was battling all this internally deep down. I still was the mom that signed up to be the room mom, would love to have my kids' friends over and watch the joy on all their faces, have endless cuddles and movie nights, create with them, take them places, and so much more. If I showed up, I put on my mask and pushed through. I tried to ignore my soul, reaching out so desperately to listen. I loved being a mom; I really did and still do. I will always treasure this part of me and our time together deeply. I feel like I am a really good mom, and it's a gift God has given me in this lifetime. I love being around and helping children. All children. I know it's a huge part of my purpose.

That's why I was deeply sad about all these tangled-up feelings, confusion, fatigue, low energy and resentments because I wasn't allowing my soul to be alive on the level it really wanted to be and had been previously in different ways and different times. I knew that I was someone who was sensitive and cared deeply about everyone around me. I felt like I was there doing all this stuff, but part of me was causing me not to be present or show up completely, and be triggered more easily. Cynical at times. Not joyful. This caused a lot of guilt for me deep down. I knew who I was, and not fully enjoying little things with my children was not that person. I just was not feeling like myself. I would try and try. It really took a toll on me. I had no idea I was experiencing burnout.

I also was allowing so much of the noise of what was expected of a mom, especially a "stay-at-home mom," into my field. I felt like I was drowning at times. It seemed so easy for everyone else, but why did I feel so different? Why can other moms feel so fulfilled and not need anything outside of motherhood? Or how can they seem like they are not struggling? I remember sitting in my car at preschool drop-off. I was struggling to get my daughter there, but I also had a two-year-old and a newborn. I watched the cars drive by the preschool parking lot, thinking, *I know one day that will be me, and I will drive by this little preschool with no preschooler to drop off. I know I will look over at the moms and look back at this exact moment, miss it, and cherish it deeply.* It brought me to tears. I also vividly remember looking at all the other moms in this moment. They were women who I thought were amazing, some who I got to know very well, and some who probably never knew I ever thought they were so amazing. I remember looking around at the moms, thinking, *How can they be fulfilled at a soul level and just be a mom? Do they feel the same way? Or is it just me? I know my family needs that more than anything right now, and I'm struggling because I love being a mom, but it feels hard for me at times. It also feels like my heart longs for something else. I had such big dreams and goals. I always have since I can remember. And here I am, living in one of the most important parts of my life, a dream I know was for my heart—my family, my purpose—and I still feel like something is missing. Where is my Joy? My energy?*

I had so much guilt and really struggled with this for so long, so if this resonates with you in any way, you are not alone. You are not alone if you are feeling the burnout of life in general. You are not crazy that you love things outside of motherhood. You are not crazy if you feel as though your heart still sings to you with dreams and other purposes, as well as your beautiful children, who I think, as parents, are one of our absolute *biggest* purposes. We should be there. We should be present. We should be filled with joy and purpose while living our life. And as you continue reading, I hope I can keep painting a picture for your heart to understand. Your heart, dreams, energy, joy, presence, and purpose are for you. And living with an alive and well heart is the best thing you can do for your family. (We will come back to all this later on!)

But there I was, diving deeper and deeper, trying to find an answer. Anything at all. Trying to get to the root cause of all my symptoms. I thought, *Come on, it's got to be a vitamin deficiency. A hormone that I am low on, right? A parasite cleanse? Therapy? Anything? ANYTHING!*

This is when, all of a sudden, out of nowhere, I received a message from someone on the IG platform I'd created so many years ago. They were a spiritual teacher and a very gifted medium. It was just a simple and kind comment on one of my posts. Nothing big, nothing telling me to reach out, nothing more than a simple "Amazing" on one of my posts. I thought, *Hmm, interesting. A medium?* I'm not even sure how or why I looked into this comment! It caught my attention for a reason, I believe. I hadn't had a reading in so long, and I only ever had a couple of readings ten years prior by the same friend of mine. Next thing you know, I listened to that nudge once again and signed up for a reading with her. She had a lot to say, and so much came up and out of me in that reading. I felt it. And I felt a little more unstuck. She also told me, "You need to go to an energy healer. Your angels are guiding you to do this." *Energy healer?*

I have never done any sort of energy healing before. I knew nothing about it at all, to be honest. Strangely enough, I had recently become curious about energy healing after seeing a comment on a blog I read about health. I took that as validation and googled for healers in my area. I felt the strong urge to seek out an energy healer!

I mean, at this point, I had tried ALL the things. I'd tried all the labs, was offered medication, did cleanses to the gut, and went on a restricted diet with try this and try that, eliminate this, start eating at this time, stop eating at this time, try this class, add this supplement, and buy this expensive vitamin. I mean I had tried everything. Also, I tried the cold shoulder to wellness in general. I needed to try something different, so why not? I had *never* done this before and had no idea what to expect. I also knew no one who had tried this before that I could ask questions of. I just kept having an urge to go and try this. If anything, I was curious about the entire process. It sounded fascinating to me, and the unknown even a little scary. I've always been a curious person and fascinated by new experiences.

I was so excited to go and try this holistic experience. I didn't know anything about it. Besides, people said, "If you are Christian, you shouldn't do that." That's all I knew. But I also knew a part of my heart was curious and wanted to find out for myself. I wanted to stop listening to all the outside noise and listen to my own heart. I will talk more about my struggles growing up and about my faith, and listening to others' opinions instead of listening to my own heart.

I thought, *How in the world is she going to even help heal my energy?* I was also wondering if I would even feel anything at all. I went to my first session with an open mind and heart. I think that's why I got so much out of that very first session. I can remember a lot about that specific day. So much. I also remember I felt connected to the healer right away. I trusted myself that I was making the right decision.

She made me feel comfortable as soon as I walked in; she explained her process and how it all worked. I was so fascinated by all this and very nervous, but I instantly felt calm as she started her session. I knew deep down I'd always been sensitive to energy, but I did not even realize or understand what that really meant before I walked into this experience.

During that first session, my life was transformed—I would never be the same. That may seem dramatic for some, as you might wonder how one tiny, little energy healing session could be life-changing. But for me, I know now it was my next step. My next puzzle piece. I really felt like there was a glass over me, and it was now shattered. I don't think I could write with words to even describe that first healing session. It was a feeling I had never felt. I felt as though I could see, hear, and feel differently. I was so much calmer; I felt more present than I had ever felt, and it was as if I knew I would never be the same. But let me tell you, I had *sooo* many questions. How could I feel so differently if I didn't eat, drink, or take medicine, and she barely touched me with her hands? I don't think she did at all, to be honest! It was all with sound, vibrations, and energy healing. *How in the world do I feel so different? My big spiritual awakening has arrived.* The biggest puzzle piece I had yet to find.

I now can see, as I am writing and looking at my path from this perspective, that I needed all those things to happen. It was all part of the plan. I needed to be angry at wellness and not feel my best. If I had, I would have continued down the same path. I would have never veered off and gone looking for answers somewhere else. I never would have gone searching for answers that I had no idea were all within me. My spiritual answers were the missing puzzle piece to wellness as a whole. I'm forever grateful for this process and the path God sent me down.

CHAPTER 2
Mind, Body, and Spirit

"Inner wisdom sets the foundation of truth, allowing expansion in optimal health over our mind, body, and spirit working as one."
– Ashley George

I was labeled as a sensitive and very shy child. I just knew what the adults were thinking and talking about without them even telling me. I just thought that everyone was like this. In high school, I knew who my best friends had crushes on before they even told me, and I could understand things without anyone saying a thing. Sometimes I knew things were going to happen before they did, and so on. What I didn't know then, but I do now, is I was sensitive because I could actually feel everyone else's energy. I most likely was reading it as well. I just had no idea about any of that. If you are reading or drawn to this book, this may resonate with you and your personality as well. If this book was something you were genuinely interested in, somehow just magically appeared to you, popped out, or was a good recommendation that made its way to your ears and heart, then yes, these words are most likely here to plant seeds within you as well.

This *knowing* kept growing as I got older, but once again, I thought I was just sensitive. To some people, this is annoying! It can be and definitely has been used against me in many ways throughout my lifetime. They use those words to put you down because your inner knowing has questions or concerns. I would often hear the words, "You are just too sensitive." To rationalize my human self and my sensitivities, I would internalize these battles and ask myself, *Why am I like this? Why do I care so much?* If I did not care so much, life would be easier! I would try to disconnect from whatever it was I was being too sensitive about. I would tell myself these things, which for years also ended up with a lot of shame and guilt within my programming. I always thought I was the problem. Quoting Taylor Swift here, "Hi, I'm the problem, it's me," was running through my head long before she wrote those lyrics. Even if I didn't allow others to know or understand this, it was what I was thinking. I thought if I could be different or more like that person—"tougher"—I would be so much happier. It would be easier for others to be with me. I would constantly tell myself this story! I want to share these internal battles I had because I see so many sensitive and shy kids these days. And I want you all to know that if you are parenting one now, there is a lot going on in their mind and heart! They also most likely are very sensitive to energy. Most kids are.

But what I didn't understand in all those moments was that I was physically feeling other people's energy and taking it as my own. I struggled to understand the difference between my own thoughts and feelings and someone else's energy. It was all tangled up, and it all landed on my heart. I didn't know then, but I do now—I'm an empath. I can feel other people's energy.

I'm bringing this up because I want to show that even though I truly had a breakthrough in that very first energy healing session, a huge one, I think I was having small breakthroughs way before I walked into that experience. A lot of us do. We just push it down and ignore it. We keep going on the path we think we are meant to be on, even if we keep pushing down that voice that tells us maybe this is not the path that serves us the best. It's comfortable not to have to change, right? This is where that ego piece comes in. That fun ego is a gem!

Our ego is the part of us that is very human. Physically human. It's the part of us that rationalizes all those deep inner-knowing moments and tells us, "No, it's not them; it really is you. Don't believe yourself because of [X, Y, Z]." Our ego likes to limit us, put us in a box, and keep us there until we are brave enough to break free in moments, if ever. Our ego can be harsh at times to ourselves. It can also be harsh or judgmental to others. We think that we can control people or situations if we can also make them believe they are their ego, not their soul's voice. Your own deep knowing, intuition, soul voice, spirit, or whatever you would like to call this, would never try to put down yourself or others. It would lead you to the best alignment of yourself! It's the voice that connects us to our spiritual self, God, our higher power, or our higher consciousness. Listening to it and understanding this is the first part of awakening.

Our ego will most likely never go away from our physical human life experience, but it's the mindset switch to understand when our ego serves us best and how to bring forward our soul's voice and lead with that most of the day. It's just like anything else; it's training. The more you train a certain muscle, the more that part of you will become stronger. It's the same thing with ego and intuition. The more we use our intuition and listen to ourselves, the more we will be stronger and more comfortable to do so.

If you are living on this planet, you have a soul, even though sometimes I question this with certain people. (We can all laugh and think of some people at this moment.) Truly, there is some evil in this world, but we all have souls, so no one is forgotten. We all have the right to be divinely connected with ourselves and God. We just *forget* how to do this. We allow so much outside noise to cover up our truth. From childhood traumas, big and small, religious traumas, outside validation, and so much more, we get covered up. Think of our hearts as a very big and bright light expanding inside of us and outside of us. Now, throw on some weeds that cover this light. The lights are still trying to poke through, but it's harder with the weeds growing over it. Every time we were hurt in our childhood, add another weed. Every time someone tells us what they would like us to do or how to be, add a weed. Every time someone tells us the only way to get to God is through fear or manipulation, add a lot of weeds. Every time someone has hurt you in any way possible, add a weed. You get the picture. We have got some yard work to do.

I feel that the very first energy healing for me was the start of my de-weeding process. I felt like my light broke through in that session in a very powerful way. Maybe that's what was truly holding me back for so long. I was going down a path that my light did not want to be on. My inner knowing was begging for me to listen, but I just wasn't listening. I didn't have the time, the patience, or the energy. I had forgotten my truth, and it was begging to come alive. My purpose was knocking at my door, and that door was coming down—it truly shattered!

The energy healing was definitely a huge part of my personal spiritual awakening, but I want people to understand that my life didn't just dramatically change overnight. I also don't want to claim this could happen for everyone. But I want to write about it because it is a part of my story. It is a part of my first-ever *de-weeding* process. It was the moment I started to think a bit differently and feel differently, a lot differently. I felt more connected with myself, calmer, and more present. I also was so much more curious about spirituality in general! I had so many questions and couldn't read enough books, listen to enough podcasts on this, and talk to anyone who was maybe a bit more "woo-woo."

To me, a spiritual awakening is the moment you realize and remember you're way more than just a physical body. And more than just always knowing that, but truly feeling this is more than we can even imagine or process with our human minds. It's the moment you feel so connected with your heart, God, and maybe everything around you. Things seem less scary in the world, and you start trusting that there is so much beauty all around us. We are all here for a reason. Our kids chose to come into the world at this time for a reason. We don't need to feel scared, drained, or heavy from all the outside noise. We need to shine brighter than ever before. We need our lights to break free and shine together. Because when we do, we all do. It's all connected. To me, that is really what a spiritual awakening is: when we are open to hearing/feeling our light and getting ourselves to the higher path. It's the path we were born and created to be on. To me, it's when you start to see things all around you a bit differently than before, and in such a beautiful way, but also through a very different lens. It's the moment you truly remember who you really are.

The more I ask others who also have had spiritual awakenings, I find they all have similar stories. A lot of times, it comes from a very rock-bottom moment—but I believe you don't have to be at rock bottom to experience this. If you are ready to shine on in your purpose, remember who you are, then start asking to be guided to your awakening and purpose. Your truth. Maybe it came through in smaller versions throughout our whole lives, but you most likely didn't let it all the way in. Or you shut it out completely. I think if you are open to it, you will break and shatter the glass that is not allowing you to shine your brightest.

You just have to ask for help from God and be brave enough to let it in and then let go of the control. Get your ego out of the way. I believe with my entire heart that if we are here now in this lifetime, we are here because we chose to come to remember. And help others do the same. It's happening a lot now and faster than we can all even realize.

The more we all feel connected to our souls, hearts, God, and our purpose, the more the world will be a different place. The more we understand our energetic bodies and footprints, we will feel more connected to our truest self. We will have fewer traumas, wars, addictions, and evil in general. Why? Because so many people feel lost and disconnected from who they truly are. They are living with their human physical self or ego and forgetting to also co-mingle with their spirit. The truth of who you really are. It's so easy to do that in today's world —feel disconnected from this part of yourself—I understand. You just have to remember that no matter what you have been through in your life, it's never too late to surrender and change paths. Let's get you on *your* correct path! Let's help you feel more connected to yourself than ever before—your authentic self.

I want to say it's beautiful to come across an awakening part of yourself and your soul. It's not always easy for many reasons, but it's beautiful. It's not easy in ways that you feel different; maybe you feel as if you are going crazy, and pieces of your old self are being washed away. Not everyone will understand this, but I promise you that if you allow your light to truly shine its brightest, this will not only serve you in all the best ways, but it will really magnify it to all those around you. In a way, the awakening is just the start, but you will continue to go down a path that dives deeper into your truth, healing, and the beauty that is within you.

Now, I can see what puzzle piece I was desperately missing: spirituality. Not because I didn't have faith before—I have always been a believer—but because I needed to find the piece within me I could not visibly see. I had to trust it was there. It was a piece that I thought I had because I had faith and had believed in God my whole life! I went to church! But I didn't realize I was thinking it was separate from me, waiting for me up in the sky. I can see myself as I write this as a woman who was picking up her pieces all along the way, not understanding what she was being guided to do, and being so hard on herself at different times and chapters in her life.

However, I can also see the pieces all coming together now. A higher power was pushing me to all these little and big experiences. I'm so incredibly grateful. I think that time I physically was not feeling like myself and couldn't find any answers was a way my spirit was trying to shake me awake. It was saying loud and clear, "Look here! The answers are not out *there* but in *here*!" Our spirits are our biggest treasures. Our biggest gifts. They are who we truly are. And if we can allow our spirits to lead the way for our physical experience here in this lifetime, our lives will be forever changed. I promise you that.

Before we end this chapter, let's pray together. Say this to yourself and come back to this if and when needed:

> *God, cover me in your beautiful white light and help me remember.*
> *I pray to you at this very moment to help me let go of all my weeds and truly start shining.*
> *I want to be able to see clearer. I want to feel present, calm, and let go of my ego self*
> *and really start listening to my higher self and you.*
> *I want you to shatter any glass that is limiting me from walking my truest path.*
> *I know I am here, created to be a child of the divine. I have a beautiful purpose.*
> *I want you to show me the way that will lead me to my heart's truth and calling.*
> *I am ready. I am here now, asking that you help and show me the way.*
> *Show me the truth. Awaken my heart to its full potential.*
> *Thank you for leading me to this very moment. I'm grateful.*

CHAPTER 3
Religion

"Religion. It's given people hope in a world torn apart by religion."
– Jon Stewart

I've debated putting an entire chapter in about religion. I'm feeling called to do so and will trust this. I also do *not* want to denigrate any religion at all, tell you it's all wrong or bad, or you failed if this part of your life means so much to you. No way! I don't have all the answers. I don't want this to appear like I'm right and everyone else is wrong. No, not even one bit! I'm just sharing my own heart's perspective. I think religion can be absolutely beautiful if that is where or how you feel connected to God. I do think there is a lot of truth inside of religion, but there is also a lot of "non-truth." There are a lot of tangled webs and routes that make us believe we are separate from God. There is a lot of fear in Religion. But that's not because of Jesus, God, Buddha, or whoever, but because of the people wanting to control the religion itself. I just want to share my story and maybe inspire others to open their hearts and minds to what I feel my heart wants to share on this topic.

I grew up in a small and beautiful Presbyterian church. My mom was the high school Sunday school teacher, and it was a very traditional Christian church. I have no crazy stories to share, no traumas, no anger, nothing besides the fact this was my first exposure to God. I went to Sunday school, and I tried to learn what they were teaching. I don't think I paid a lot of attention, to be honest, but I was doing what I was being taught. I didn't feel moved or close to God, though. It felt like the stories and lessons I was being taught seemed so far removed, and I couldn't possibly understand it with my childhood brain. I remember having questions—lots of them.

Since I was little, I have believed in Jesus with my whole heart. I felt like He was my friend and different from what was being taught at times. I always felt like He was the best kind of friend you could imagine. He would not judge but would listen with His entire heart, which was completely open. I began talking to Jesus at a very young age. At times, this was so confusing to me because of how others, in different times or situations in my life, viewed or used Jesus—as a cover to be judgmental, to instill fear in others, to feel superior to others, or to justify their anger. I always thought, *Hmmm, I don't feel like he's like that.* I felt like there was a disconnect somewhere. *Is it me?* I would think. *Or was it them?*

It's interesting for me to go back and remember these things now with this perspective that I'm writing from. I never felt like God was in my heart or a part of me; I felt like He was a man in the sky dictating who got in and who did not. That is how He was presented to me through our church, which can be scary at times for a young child. It's a lot to think about and process, depending on how they are being told the story of who God is and how to get to know Him. Some people truly are taught that only certain people are worthy enough to know Him at the end of their life. This is terrifying to believe in your heart. I understand why people can feel so scared to live in a way that someone else is controlling and dictating for them to make sure their connection to God is secure. And to me, that is very sad.

My parents got divorced in middle school. My dad went to an evangelical church after this, and my mom went to a non-denominational Christian church. I think it was early in high school when I truly started to feel more connected through my mom's church. (My dad also now attends a non-denominational church). I loved the pastor's stories and the way he gave us relatable and usable ways to take the scripture and apply it to our everyday lives. I also really loved the music. I think this is where I really started to feel connected to God and what that really even meant to me. We were not super involved with this church, but it opened my heart and eyes to wanting to stick with this route moving forward. I knew deep down there was some truth to this way of teaching the Bible. I felt like I knew deep within that the teaching about God's love and how to use this in your everyday world deeply resonated with me.

I stuck with more of the non-denominational churches moving forward. If I'm being completely honest, I never felt super connected to any of them. But I was so thankful for each of them and the role they played at that time. I have tried so many over the years, because I knew my faith was important to me. That's where I struggled and got so conflicted! (Thanks, ego!) I felt that if I wanted this to be a part of my life, I had to find a church, go every week, and be a good "Christian." Otherwise, what was the point, right? I would try and try and try again, always finding something that didn't fit quite exactly right deep within. There was always some disconnection from the context or message being presented—a feeling. I felt like maybe we weren't getting the whole truth. It's as if my heart was saying there is something deeper, and we are missing it.

Fast forward to being married and having a family, and this guilt got even worse. I thought, *We have to find the right church for our family! Our kids have to grow up with God in their life. I don't want them to not know about God. We have to find a church that fits us all so they can feel the connection and understand who God is.* We tried a lot. We found a couple we did like and would attend, but once again, I still felt like there was something missing.

My husband grew up Catholic. So, that was in the mix as well. It was conflicting for all of us at times. How did we teach our kids about the Bible? God? Religion? What did we really believe?

My husband is actually a good example of someone growing up in a certain religion, which I think made him feel separate from God. (That's his personal experience, but I will not speak for him.) He didn't know how to feel God. He would go to church a couple of times a year for the major holidays, go through the correct actions and steps, and move on. He didn't really think about it much more than those brief encounters. He did love asking the bigger questions, thinking outside of the box, and that's why he was so open to trying some new churches. I was thankful for this.

This was when even more guilt started to settle in because I wondered how I was ever going to teach my children about God and religion. I felt like I just could not find something or a church that deeply resonated with my heart, but we continued to show up so we could expose our children to God. It was so important to me!

During Covid and after Covid, I didn't focus on it so much, and it felt so far away from my heart at the time, to be honest. I felt so disconnected from my own inner belief system. What do I believe? I didn't know what to think, believe, or trust anymore. This did make me awaken to the sense of thinking a bit differently. I asked different questions and started looking through a different lens in a way that maybe I didn't do before as much. At that time, I found myself questioning things I normally wouldn't—not just about religion, but about everything happening in the world. This was setting me up for what was to come on a deep level that I had no idea was there. It's as if I was deeply trusting myself, even if I had become so disconnected from what I thought was God.

Fast forward to early 2022, and I am having my true awakening to my spiritual self. I not only felt different that day, but I felt more connected to God, angels, and Jesus than ever before. Even though that truly made me feel crazy at times. I'm not going to lie! I remember thinking, *Can I tell anyone what I actually am feeling, sensing, hearing deep from within my own heart? Can I tell them I think we may have this a little wrong?* I wanted to connect and talk to anyone at the time with a similar mindset. Anyone. I read books of all kinds, listened to podcasts, and looked up anyone I thought could help or help me validate my own deep truths. I read books on angels, history books on Jesus, and researched many religions. I thought it was all fascinating and all so connected in such a bigger way—way more than we all may think or realize. I felt there were truths in all of it, together. We are ALL connected.

This is the part that I promise I won't tell you, and your religion or belief system is wrong. That is not the message I want to spread. I do want to bring the truth to light, though. I want you to know that whatever you were taught or how you feel, all of our truths and connections to God come straight from our own hearts. We do not need anyone else outside of us to secure a closer relationship with God. You have the control over that, no one else. People can lead you or inspire you, but ultimately, it's your own connection that will strengthen that bond or not. We do not need to be worthy enough of His love. I promise you that you are already deeply loved. Also, your connection to God is within you. No one but you has the power to turn that on or off. They don't have magic, energetic scissors that can cut your connection off. Only you get to decide that.

In a way, my awakening is a huge expansion of the faith that I always have had. It doesn't need to be one choice or the other. I understand not everyone will agree with that. I didn't need to search outside of me for this connection. I feel it within me. I don't need to label what I call my connection to God or what religion it fits into. If I had to, I would still say Christian or Christ consciousness. But I feel when I put a label on it, other people don't feel welcome. Can you feel that? As soon as you label your route to God, it changes because your ego starts to believe that your connection is the only right way and that others are wrong. That contradicts what I'm trying to share. No matter how you want to label it, it's your own. And the person next to you has their own. And so on.

I feel strongly connected to the angels, Jesus, Mary Magdalene, Mother Mary, and many other divine beings from all world religions. So whatever you want to call it, it's beautiful and full of love. I know with every cell in my body we are absolutely divinely guided. We have angels all around us who want to help us. They also do not think you need to label yourself to grow your connection to your divine self or God. They understand all the ways we have been taught and guided in our connections and truths. They just want us to realize that our connection can be so much stronger when we internalize our belief systems and go straight to the connection instead of allowing outside validation to get in the way. They don't want us to fear that connection to our divine self. They don't want us to feel so much shame or guilt because someone is telling us the "rules" to get to God. Life can be so much easier if we don't fear that part of us and if we allow our divine guidance all around us in.

They are here to help us! They want you to hear the music that plays loudly from deep within your truest heart's desires, God-given gifts, and talents, and they want you to know and understand they are here to help all of you gain a stronger connection. It's possible for all of us to come together and recognize we are so much more similar in the way we connect to God when we break free from the mess that can hold us back and the chains or the misinformation given to us so long ago. It's time to really dive deeper from within and raise your consciousnesses, expand your faith, and look at the bigger picture. It's *your* time to remember your own truths. Your own heart. Your own connection. It is absolutely beautiful. I also deeply believe you can do all this inside of the beautiful religion that you love.

I am going to quote a few lines by Father Richard Rohr. I highly recommend his book, *The Universal Christ*. It dives so much deeper into all this, and I felt so much truth in that book deep within my own heart. He has done profound research on religion, questioning translations at times, and the history behind them. More importantly, he is a spiritual thinker, curious, and a God-loving soul. I find his work absolutely fascinating. In *The Universal Christ*, Father Rohr writes, "We were largely taught what to believe, instead of how to believe. We had faith in Jesus, often as if He were an idol, more than sharing the expansive faith of Jesus, which is always humble and patient (Matthew 11:25) and can be understood only by the humble and patient. We can begin to understand that the Christ Mystery is not something we need to prove or even can prove, but a broad field that we can recognize for ourselves when we see in a contemplative way, which often will seem more symbolic and intuitive than merely rational, a more nodule mystery than anything that offers us more binary choices as a false shortcut to wisdom."

When we really just pause and think about this for a minute. It can be profound. Before we came into this world we were spirit. After we leave this world we are spirit. Why would we believe that God would punish us for connecting to our spirit (our divinity) or our spiritual gifts while we are here in this lifetime? Why do we think God would want us to not remember who we authentically are? Or that He would want us to feel separate from this part of ourselves? That's who we truly are and always will be. It's the real us. The most authentic parts of who we are. Don't you think He would want us to be connected to this part of ourselves and the divine wisdom around us, instead of fearing it or labeling it as bad, "darkness," evil, etc.? Or insisting that we are separate from it, and that the only way to be worthy of God's acceptance is through rules, ego, and guilt? It just doesn't make sense. I think our human brains make this a way bigger deal than it really is because it's been passed down with fear and manipulation for centuries through structures and systems telling us the right way to get to God. If we all knew how powerful we are from within—how much love is inside of us—we would need a lot less outside of us. YOU are the church. It's within you. You can lead not only yourself with this love but also teach and lead your family to do the same.

We also have to remember there is a HUGE universe out there— HUGE. We will never understand this with our human minds, either. There are other life forms, dimensions, realms, things and words I don't even know how to type and know nothing about. It's massive. If we believe God created everything, I think He would want us to experience our full potential. He would want us to be curious and explore our full power. Ask questions! Learn and grow, expand your knowledge, have conversations with people who may think differently than you. He would NOT want us to feel trapped, limited, or controlled. The universe is massive, just like the potential you have within you is massive. Not limited.

I believe He also would not want us to feel superior or judgmental to others because of our routes to God—because that's not unconditional love. Why would He give us life and then want to have us spend our entire lives trapped with fear, shame, and guilt in honor of Him? That is NOT unconditional love. This is what never made sense to me. Now, from this perspective, it's like everything in me knows that is not true. God is LOVE. He wants you to know the real you. LOVE is what will change not only you but everyone around you. Love will change the world. Because that is God. And that is YOU.

CHAPTER 4

Our Souls

"A happy soul is the best shield for a cruel world."
– Atticus

How unbelievably fascinating are our souls? Regardless of your beliefs attached to them, it's undeniably interesting. I don't think we will ever fully grasp this concept with our human self. It's too magical to understand! But what I have really come to understand and learn is fascinating. I believe in what feels right in my heart, even if I can never prove it. I have faith.

Our souls are a part of us that we cannot see. We must just believe in them. It's where trusting ourselves and having faith play a part. That connection to the higher power goes straight from our soul to the source/God/higher power. Scientists have proven our hearts have an electromagnetic field that goes from our heart to the outside of our body. They can measure it up to 3ft outside of our body. Our hearts are actually the largest rhythmic electromagnetic field in the entire body. They say the heart's energetic field is 60 times greater in amplitude than the electrical activity generated by the brain. So, when I'm constantly talking about our hearts and souls in this book, I truly believe the energy our heart produces connects us to the spirit of who we are. That is the real us. And it links us to each other. We can feel each other's energy. That is not just "woo-woo" talk these days—it's proven. That's why I think connecting to our hearts is so powerful. I think it's connecting us to our souls.

In one of my absolute favorite books, *Mary Magdalene Revealed* by Meggan Watterson, she describes so beautifully what I deeply sense is true. This book goes through the lost scripture from Mary Magdalene herself, which is fascinating and I highly recommend this book if you have yet to read it.

Mary describes in her scripture that the "eye of the heart" is what will save us from the false self (the ego). "And in that moment of recognition, we save ourselves from the self that was never real to begin with. This is when we see with the eye of the heart. It's about acquiring a vision that allows us to see what has always been within us." Mary also goes on to share throughout this book about how this can transform your entire life when you are open to this inner wisdom deep within your own heart.

I personally feel like this is the only thing we need to be "saved" from. Our own misguided thinking. Our own negativity. The ego self. Feeling separate from God and our divine self. I wholeheartedly believe this is what Jesus' teachings were as well—trying to show what was possible for us while we are living in human form. Trying to teach us that "the kingdom of God is within you" (Luke 17:21). Your own heart. A heart full of love and wisdom. I think being open to this part of you is what so many of us are searching for.

But so many of us look outside of us for that validation of truth. I really believe Jesus and Mary were trying to show what was possible while we are living on earth with this connection open from within us. I don't think He was trying to set up rules or systems to keep us feeling trapped or separate from this part of us—or each other. He did not want us to feel limited or disconnected from our own power. He was teaching, "What I shall do, you shall do better." He was teaching what was possible for all of us with our own energy and God's connection.

Understanding this part of you and not fearing your own truth is when miracles can truly happen. Jesus may have been one of the best spiritual teachers to have ever walked Earth. But I don't think he wanted to create an entire life where you feel shame, guilt, or unworthiness in his name. Or judgment upon others or feeling superior to others because you pray to Jesus. He wanted to teach us that when you see with the eye of the heart, you are powerful beyond doubt. Because you are full of love for yourself and others. You are connected to the truth of who you are.

We all want to understand why we are here. What is the point or purpose of our lives? Why do we come to Earth and live a life in the first place? Why do we find ourselves asking why a God or higher power would allow so much suffering here for so many? There are endless questions surrounding souls. I also believe there are endless answers, knowledge, and wisdom that our souls contain. There is information and wisdom that we are allowed to tap into, live with, and bring forward in our everyday lives.

I believe when our time has come to transition to the other side, our physical body dies, but the real us, our souls, continues on in our journey. We never really die. We hold on to our experiences, relationships, and knowledge that this life brought to us. That IS the purpose of life. To grow, expand, learn, connect, and heal. Our purpose is actually pretty simple; we are here to *live* in physical form. When we think about it from this perspective, it can start to shift our everyday reality into the most beautiful heaven-on-earth perception. We get to experience *life*. How amazing is that? From connection with other humans to love, romance, food, laughter, sadness, joy, and creation, it never ends. The simplest of things are wonderful, like putting our feet in the sand and being able to feel it, being able to taste an amazing dinner we prepared with love, and laughing with friends about memories and experiences we have shared.

This is what I think my spirit was trying to remind me so desperately of at a time when I couldn't understand what was happening. *Life* itself is the purpose. We don't need to chase after the next big thing, career, goal, success, or lack of. Once we understand that living is truly a big part of our purpose, those things come along with it easily. We absolutely can still have goals and dreams. We just start to flow more energetically and listen to ourselves. Trust ourselves. Our path. Our dreams. And we start getting ourselves there. We set ourselves up to walk the path of our absolute highest dreams and goals once we start trusting ourselves, believing in ourselves, and allowing our most authentic selves to lead the way. Don't get me wrong, some people do have big dreams and goals! That IS a part of their purpose in this lifetime.

Watching our children experience their own lives and have so many experiences for the first time is such a great example of what we all forget. We forget that being human is a gift. It is simply a huge part of our purpose. We are meant to experience life, whatever that may look like and mean for you, but if we can remember at times that the simplicity of life is actually what I think we are looking for a lot of the time—that true joy and feeling alive in general, and the thing that so many of us go searching for and long for. It seems to come so naturally to kids. They are our best teachers a lot of the time. Watching them, experiencing life with them, and most importantly, listening to them, we can see they hold so much power and purpose in life from within. They are still so connected to God. And their hearts. When they are little, they don't know anything different from being connected to God. It's when they realize or have been taught they are separate, like so many of us, that they start to become aware of what they need to do to fit in. And fitting in looks different for every child. When we start shutting down their natural superpowers, we can start to see the small changes of the complex and simple awe of life start melting away from their childhood.

We have all gone through this—every single one of us. When we start to listen to our ego, we become more aware we aren't just this being of light. Our brain starts noticing we are separate. I absolutely love Dr. Wayne Dyer's definition of ego. He believes ego stands for "Edge God

Out." There couldn't be a better way to explain our ego! I think the more we as parents are aware of this, the more we can start to help keep those gifts and connections open. We can reassure them their lights are never separate from God, let them always feel connected to who they really are, be who they are, and guide them to their own purpose. Their own eye of the heart. We should let them lead with their soul and divine self instead of telling them who they are and what they should do to fit in. We should allow children to have imaginary friends, who might often be their angels, spirit guides, or something similar. Simply put, children are amazing, and we should be learning from them. Instead of silencing them, conforming them to societal expectations, or placing shame and guilt on their consciousness because of our own unrealistic expectations, let's learn from them. Let's grow with them. Let's heal because of them. Let's not take away their superpowers, their voices, their emotions, their heart. They are too important, too magical, and it all cycles around. Sometimes, I think we've got it all backward.

When our soul transitions, we are not bringing our physical body with us. This makes our physical life even more of a gift. It is one to treasure, experience, and really be thankful for. Sometimes, when I really sit with this and think about it, it really does make the simplest of things bring tears to my eyes. (Yes, I am a sensitive empath here, *ha!*) Watching my children is such a good example of this. From watching my son hit a home run on his baseball team to my littlest just picking a dandelion from the ground, saying, "Here, Mommy, this is for you," or my oldest daughter singing and dancing her heart out on stage, one of her favorite things to do, these moments that are so simple, yet make us feel physically human. They get to *feel* their soul in their physical body, but so do we if we take the time and are open to appreciating those little things. Watching our children feel so human in those simplest of moments also makes us feel so alive. It's all connected. It all has *purpose*.

This is also a great reminder about how important our physical bodies really are. They really are the temple for our spirits. And the better we care for them, the better we can hear and feel connected to our spirit. How do we want to treat our temples? Do we say harsh things about our temples? Allow them to never feel good enough? Feed our temples poison? Or can we shift our mindset to allow ourselves to start connecting our bodies and spirit together?

I think a lot of us have a hard time really fully being grounded in our bodies, whether we are consciously aware of this or not. This can stem from so many things throughout our lifetime where we disconnect or want to control our physical bodies. We start to forget we are the spirit and not our body. We put so much pressure on who we are and only allow ourselves to be physical. We don't allow ourselves to feel connected to our soul. We disconnect. This is why mind, body, and spirit are so important. They really are. It's the shift you make to really allow yourself to have your spirit/soul take over your body and lead the way. When we allow just our physical self to lead the way and our spirit is desperately trying to break free, we can start having physical problems and symptoms.

Our bodies are amazing. They are incredible. And they can heal themselves on so many levels. We just can't forget that our spirit and bodies need to co-mingle. They need each other to live in optimal health. Shutting down one for the other will lead to problems. But when we embrace the beauty of both and take care of both, that's when the magic starts happening. We really do start to live with our soul self, our divine self, leading the way. We start healing. When we can really step into optimal health and start to heal things we never thought possible, we really start to believe in ourselves. We can start showing gratitude toward our physical body. I mean, we wouldn't even be here if we didn't have a body, so taking care of it is so important. Being grateful for our bodies is so important. If this is something you need to work on yourself, remember this is in baby steps. Embrace small changes to your mindset each day. Work on changing your negative thoughts to small, grateful things about yourself physically. It's easy for us, especially women (but I know so many men struggle with this as well), to be so hard on ourselves because of our physical bodies.

We live in a world where all we see, hear, and know is about how we are supposed to look physically. I think it's changing, but it's definitely still there. So, when we shift our mindsets, I'm grateful for my physical body. I'm grateful I get to take care of *me* this way. I'm grateful for beautiful food that makes me *feel* good. I'm grateful for movement that makes me *feel good*. I'm grateful I'm strong and healthy, and I feel *alive!* When we shift our mindset, we really can start living with our body, mind, and spirit all working together, understanding our energetic body and our physical body. This is when you will start to truly transform your life and health.

This is what my physical body was trying to tell me when I was going through all my changes. It was trying to stop me dead in my tracks to say, "Hey, you have put so much attention into your physical health, but you're forgetting about your spirit." It was almost like I became a robot and was doing all the things the outside world was telling me to do so I could be "healthy": Do all the things so I can feel physically healthy. Do all the things so I can be a good mom. Do all the things so I can be a good wife. Do all the things that led me further and further away from my own soul. I listened to the outside noise and everyone else's advice, ignoring my own inner voice. I went through the motions, convincing myself I was connected and taking care of myself, but I had forgotten that none of it reflected who I truly was at my core. I am a soul. A divine being. I have a purpose. I came here with a plan, but I kept walking further and further away from it. So, my physical body started to shut down in different ways, and I did not feel like myself. It showed me signs about how and what I needed to do to help heal myself. I'm so glad I listened. I'm glad I dug deep to find my root cause.

I put so much value on listening to all the outside noise about what it takes to be a good mom, what a woman who is healthy should look like, what I need to do to make sure our marriage is a good one, and what I need to do to make sure everyone thinks we have it all together (when we are a house full of beautiful chaos with three young children, *ha!*) when all this was the complete opposite of who I really am. But none of that means that I don't care about those things. Here is the conflicting part. I deeply care about all those things. I deeply care about being a good mom. I deeply care about my physical health. I deeply care about my marriage and my career. I think the disconnect happens when we turn to all the outside noise and validation from those things and when we only look at what others tell us and only listen to the advice about how to get those things from other people.

When we listen to everyone else besides ourselves, we forget that we already have all the answers inside of us. They are already all there! There is literally nothing that we don't already have within us. When we can flip to that mindset and let the spirit lead the way in all these areas, *Wow* can happen along with true miracles. Do you know how we can do that? It's not easy, but remember, it's all in baby steps. For me, it was surrounding control over all these situations and the outcomes attached to them. Yes, you heard me. Surrendering our control. That one didn't come easy for me. I like to be in control of myself and the outcomes attached to whatever it may be. Thanks anxiety!

When we continuously allow so-and-so to tell you how to be a good mom, partner, employee, or wife, that's when we let other people take our power. *None* of that is true. In all those moments, we are allowing ourselves to believe what we are seeking is outside of ourselves, and we allow our power to be taken from us again and again. We continue to search for happiness, joy, and health. All of it. We feel so separate from it all, search for answers, and listen to the outside noise, trying anything to make us feel alive and well. We allow our soul selves to be completely disconnected from our truth. Our inner wisdom. Our answers. We allow our lights to be dimmed and cover them with more weeds.

It doesn't mean we don't value what others say; it simply is a reminder to us all that we can hear anything, but we feel the truth. That does not mean words can't emotionally hurt us, but they are emotions and not our real selves! We can physically feel the truth. We just ignore it a lot of the time and cover it up, letting our emotions get the best of us. Believe me, I can relate! When someone says something to us, and it hurts our feelings, whether it's true or not, it's hard to step out of emotion and into truth. But the truth is always there. It never disconnects from you. You know who you are and what is true and what is not. It doesn't mean our feelings will never get hurt again, but it means we know our value, our worth, and our power. And we do things to make us feel good and more connected to ourselves. So, when words are spoken to hurt us, we can come back to our own inner strength. We also have fewer relationships that emotionally hurt us. Why? Because we are connected to our power and our truth. Why would we ever want to be around people who constantly want to bring us down?

That's why listening to certain words of truth and words spoken from other people's hearts can resonate and inspire us deeply. When we are connected to our divine self, our own truth, when we have the eye of the heart open, we feel deeply. We know what is true and what does not seem to be resonating with us. We don't let the outside noise dim our lights any longer. We shine brighter than ever before. And when we shine brighter than ever before, we are washed over with so much love, peace, and joy. It washes away the fear. Anyone can say anything about us and who we are, but we don't allow that to define who we truly are. We know the truth. And we will then watch motherhood, marriage, our careers, our relationships, and everything else shine brighter, too. Why? Because we don't control the outcomes. We let what was meant to be washed away wash away. We let all that anxiety that was piled so high because we were so worried about an outcome that hasn't even happened wash away. For no reason, everything built up in our minds we let get washed away.

Once we trust in ourselves, our divine path—the purpose we were meant for—must guide us. We must listen to ourselves. We can see beautiful and healthy relationships walk into our lives. We can start to see the magic of trusting our souls. We can see our worth and our own value. Our true self. When we have pushed the ego aside, we can tell the difference when it comes back into play. When we detach from any outcome and allow our hearts/souls to lead, we really watch the magic happen. That may not always be easy. Relationships can wash away, you can lose a job, and so on, but maybe it was supposed to happen so you can be led to the path that your heart has been trying to get you to for so long—your highest path yet. We know what our hearts want and what we are capable of. We just forget. We get covered with all the weeds and the outside heaviness of the world.

When we truly surrender to God and let our soul take over, let God take over, our life is forever changed. One of my favorite quotes that has such a true and deeper meaning to me now that I can really see so much of my own truth is what Jesus told us in Matthew 19:26, *"With man this is impossible, but with God all things are possible."* I feel like Jesus was trying to explain a similar context. If we disconnect and become just a robot or think we are just physical beings, we aren't incorporating the mind, body, and spirit in our own temple. Things won't be possible with this disconnect. When we come alive and understand who we really are and how powerful we truly are, when we really and truly awaken to the realization we are connected to God and He is within us, all things are possible. With that connection open inside of your own temple, watch out; your life is about to transform. With God, all things are possible.

CHAPTER 5

Our Human Life; Let's Help Each Other Be Human

"Our greatest ability as humans is not to change the world, but to change ourselves."
– Gandhi

We have talked a lot about our spirit leading the way so far, and you may be thinking, *Well, that's great that you say life is the purpose, but just living doesn't make us money. It doesn't do the laundry, make dinner, or clean all those dishes, Ashley! It doesn't pay the bills!*

Here is where I'm going to bring our mindset back in along with our spirit and truly combine the mind, body, and spirit philosophy. If we can start connecting to that part of us, our spirit/soul, and really allow our spirit to lead the way, I do think all of that will change. Once we live with our soul connection to ourselves again and turn that light back on, I think you will find that the simplest of things seem to create more meaningful effects. You make dinner because you get to cherish that time and nourish yourself and your family. (Mindset shift.) You're helping all the temples of the family! You do the day-to-day tasks because it creates an energy within the household that uplifts everyone. (Mindset shift.) Kids thrive on less chaos and more organization. It's all energy-related!

It's not just the mindset shift, but also understanding how powerful we are and how we are creating our realities. From our thoughts we think each day, to the laundry piles, to the food we eat. Everything has energy, even the tiny little LEGOs we all have stepped on as parents. And energy holds a frequency. So, when energy is clear, we all can feel it, especially the kids. Reminder: this is not about being perfect, it's about doing things that make your energy feel good. So your entire family's energy feels good, balanced, and clear. My house is far from always being perfect. But I have created little systems and set up organization to clear the energy.

I'm sharing this because, as someone who is super sensitive to energy, I have learned this really matters to me. And I think it does for kids as well. I don't like energy (or things) being all over the place for too long. For whatever reason, I can tell it heightens my anxiety. I feel more triggered and less motivated. I have learned this is because it's all energy-related. Everything has energy, whether you want to believe it or not! I'm not saying to not let kids be creative or make messes (that's a part of curiosity and exploring their own energy), but I'm saying I have built little systems where I can easily put things back and so can they when we are all done making the 100 messes a day we all make. The energy of the household matters! Clear out anything you don't use, wear, etc. It's holding onto old energy, and you want the fresh, balanced, calming energy around you each day. You will feel lighter, clearer, and calmer.

When we are in a space of lighter and calmer energy, I think we can listen to our hearts more. We feel more clarity—less heaviness. This is so important for our children as well. They are incredibly sensitive to energy!

When we start truly living in our hearts, we really start to flow into an energetic state when we let our soul lead the way, and we genuinely start to see magic happen in our everyday lives. Once we open ourselves to the love of who we really are, we pour love out all around us in our day-to-day purposes. It's important, and it matters. We can all feel energy, whether we think so or not, especially our kids. Once we really understand how our energetic bodies work, what lights them up, or what drains them, we can start to flow better.

This doesn't mean that I think life becomes perfect or that we don't have human moments where we still don't love doing laundry (*me*), or the dishes, (*me*), or we never feel tired or human again. No! It's just realizing how important it is to take care of our own energy, and the energy of our households in many different ways. That will GIVE you energy! I promise!

When our spirit and our soul are filled up by doing things that we love or are passionate about, the day-to-day seems less daunting. You also know that your day-to-day tasks are incredibly purposeful. They help everyone around us tremendously. We either fill that with negative energy or we fill it with love. Mindset shift. Soul shift. All of a sudden, you're a Disney princess singing to the birds because you are so happy to be cleaning your house. Ha-ha, just kidding! Sorry, I had to throw that in there. Maybe that is something you love to do, and maybe that is something you do not love to do. I will never be the Disney princess singing because I'm cleaning. No matter how much energy work I do. (*Haha!*)

Either way, give yourself more grace. Take back your power, shift your mindset, and ask for help if and when you need it. Don't place unrealistic expectations on yourself any longer. Free your spirit! At times, we all need to help each other with day-to-day tasks. I think that's by giving each other grace. And also not placing unrealistic expectations on others or ourselves in the first place. When we place a value on people by how many day-to-day tasks they did or did not accomplish, we should ask ourselves, why does that make us feel superior to others? Or let others feel shame or guilt because we accomplished more? Some days will be easier than others. We are human! But we have to remember that doing the tasks that make our own energy and our household energy feel better on a daily basis are very important. I know sometimes it's the last thing we want to do at certain times, but it deeply matters, for all of you. It will help you overall productive energy on a every single day basis, if you get up and move. Get things done and accomplished. You are clearing energy and balancing your energy for everyone. If you feel stuck and heavy right now, take this as motivation to declutter. Clean. Clear out old energy!

We are all different. We have strengths and weaknesses, and we value certain things while others we do not. I believe our day-to-day tasks can flow more easily when we approach them with a positive mindset. We do these things out of love for ourselves and our families. It's an important mindset shift. If I'm being honest, it doesn't always come easily to me, but when I truly practice it, it works. Just like any other muscle group, the more we work on it, the easier it is to strengthen that muscle. Muscle memory is real, and our mind is a muscle. We can strengthen our minds, expand them, and even change them. We can learn, grow, and heal our minds. It's all possible with your spirit leading the way! Don't ever feel overwhelmed by this, or guilt or shame if you still hate doing day-to-day tasks. Baby steps!

I also think once we get back our own power, we care less about what we are supposed to do or how we get certain things done. You return your worth. You start speaking more. What is working for you, and what is not? How can others in the family help you? And how can all of us humans start helping each other? Start clearing the energy in your space. What makes you feel good, and what does not? Remember, everything is energy. Our day-to-day environment definitely affects our overall energy. Our mood. Everything. If we are consciously aware of it or not, it truly does. It's all connected.

I don't believe motherhood or fatherhood is meant to be done alone. I think we've become disconnected from this part of our culture. Consider the rising rates of postpartum depression, the increasing anxiety and depression levels, and the growing number of prescriptions across all stages of motherhood and parenting. Look at the heartbreaking suicide rates among men, which continue to climb higher and higher. These numbers are just as concerning for teens and young adults. It's all so heartbreaking to me.

I believe this is because so many of us feel deeply disconnected from who we truly are. We feel lost, weighed down, heavy and have allowed so much outside noise to infiltrate our lives in countless forms. For a moment, let's go back to the very beginning of life itself—children.

Bringing other souls into this world is one of the most important purposes of all our lives as parents. That should be cherished. I think it would help society, in general, to have children being raised by mothers and fathers who took time to not only heal themselves before they become parents but had a community around them to help when they could not even help themselves. It's hard for mothers, when they are so sleep-deprived, to manage all the things society has placed on them. We don't know any better. We think, *Well, this is how it is. This is what it means to be a mom.* And we often think to ourselves, *I have to push through. If I can't do this like so-and-so, I must be doing something wrong. It's me, not society. Something is wrong with me.* Welcome to motherhood guilt.

Imagine the world we would live in if we placed value on mothers' healing and parents being with their children in that first year of life and continued to value parents well beyond that first year. If we put a value on cherishing a woman who just gave birth and made sure to help set up resources for her and the family to thrive, not just survive, that would be amazing. Imagine if we gave them information on actual healing. Imagine if we surrounded the parents and child with so much love and just showed up because we wanted to help and serve in any way. If we can break through our ego on both ends and just come to serve with actual human love and receive the love as well, for the mother's soul and the child's soul, to me, that is what God's love is really all about. It is helping each other *be human.*

Helping other humans be humans in all different ways is what is needed. We can look at other humans and are quick to judge them. What we forget is we all have stories. We all have childhoods. We all have different paths. We all have our lights turned on brightly, or maybe we have a lot of weeds covering up those very bright lights from within us. Keeping us very disconnected from the truth of who we really are.

Next time you see someone where you just feel like they may need help in any way, shape, or form, I encourage you to do so. Maybe it's a friend who just had a baby and needs sleep or a warm meal. Maybe it's a new mother who is feeling lonely and would love a conversation. Maybe it's a father who needs his own emotions validated, a man who looks hungry, a child who looks like they could use a hug or a meal themselves, or a simple smile and a heart hug. (Saying something kind to them to make them feel good). A single parent in desperate need of help, a child who has been placed in foster care, or help clean a space for a friend who seems overwhelmed. There are SO many ways all of us can help each other be human. You never know what other humans are walking through. Sometimes, I look out into the world and think, *Why do some of us forget that it can really be hard to be human?*

We won't know until we try. It takes people and courage to step out of what is normal and pursue their soul's path. It is not always easy to do this. I understand this myself—believe me. I'm writing a book on souls, angels, and God, for goodness sake, so I get it. I understand that stepping off the path that everyone else is screaming in the right way can be hard. It's confusing, conflicting, and scary. But when we remember that part of surrendering to God or the universe and trusting in ourselves, we won't have anything to be scared of. We have our power back.

When we really understand, we are being divinely guided and called to take whatever path it may be. Yes, it might look different than other people's paths, but you have to tune into your own truth. God would never put you on a path to hurt yourself or others. That is not God. He may push you outside your comfort zone to learn and grow, but He will never guide you to bring harm into the world. If you are being guided to bring harm into the world or any negativity, control, or instill fear, that is not God. It's most likely your ego. Once we really feel connected to our spirit again, our own power, it's less scary to veer off the straight path.

We can be the voices to create the change. I encourage you to turn that light on and stand in your power. Let's change the world. Let's help humanity. Let's help each other. Let's help the children. Like I keep saying, it really is all connected. Let your spirit lead the way! Changing the world starts with your own connection to your own healing. I also think it starts with us remembering we are all human. Let's not make it so hard for each other to be human and do things because it's the right thing to do.

Working on your energy/soul self helps everything, including the nervous system. Tremendously! Meditation has been proven to calm our sympathetic nervous system. When we meditate and really connect to that part of us, to God, we are deactivating the sympathetic nervous system and then turning on the parasympathetic branch. Studies have found this, over time, helps reduce anxiety, depression, stress, and overall pain. To me, this is why our spiritual side is so important to our overall health. It helps the nervous system, which so many of us don't understand, and is the major cause of all our triggers, our noise overload, illness, and so much more. That is so important when we become a mother or a father. We need to incorporate healing into the nervous system. Awakening and realizing we have the ability to help heal this part of us already within us is amazing and nothing short of a miracle. I don't think this needs to be hours and hours of meditation. I think you should become aware of this side of you first, then take a few minutes each day to connect to this side of you. It's life-changing.

Being human is hard, guys. I don't think it was ever intended or created to be easy. We came to experience lessons. And I feel passionately about creating different dynamics around being human. Parents healing themselves is so important because we can create the shift that truly changes humanity—healed parents raising healed children. It's not giving our power away thinking it's one person outside of us that can come save and change the world. It's not going to be a political leader, a religious leader, a parent, or anyone outside of you. We give so much power to thinking it's going to be this one person that saves everything. I think it starts with us. We have the power to change the world by healing ourselves, trusting ourselves, using our discernment, and creating an environment that sets up unconditional love for the next generation—helping our communities by being loving and non-judgmental humans to other humans and giving grace to each other! Less ego, more heart!

Like I keep saying, it's not about being perfect; there is no such thing. It's about doing the work so we can show our kids that it's possible as well. They can live a life full of love and know the power that lies within their own heart. We can lead by example.

There will always be lessons we are going through in life. We came to overcome those lessons and grow and expand. We came to really understand who we are. Why are we here? We came to remember that part of us. And I think when we connect to that part of us, that soul part, it's the first step in a major transformation of your life. It's your shift to awakening and seeing from a different perspective. When we can have compassion not only for ourselves but for all humans, and when we step out of our ego and into our spirit—our true selves—we can better help each other simply by being human. The old ways are not working. It's time to create new ones from love and truth.

CHAPTER 6
Old Souls

"You have to keep breaking your heart until it opens."
– Rumi

I believe that since our soul never dies, it will continue to experience life in many forms. I don't think our souls have a beginning or an end. They are infinite. They continually want to expand. They don't want to be shut off or limited. I don't think it's possible for our souls to do so. We came here to expand and grow; that is why our soul pushes us —if we are brave enough to listen—to different experiences in our lives. I think we are all at different and various ages; yes, soul ages. So many of us throw out the term and label kids, friends, and even pets as old souls. I feel like we are saying those things for a reason, even if we didn't really put much more thought into why we are saying it in the first place. We know deep down they are an old soul. They have been here before and may even be coming back one day.

So, yes, I do believe we have past lives and future lives. If we believe our soul never dies and is in heaven for an infinite time, that is hard for my brain to even conceptualize! I think our soul does return to have more lifetimes, to grow and expand. It learns, gathers experiences, knowledge, and gifts, and treasures them. It holds onto all these things forever. It's who we are. I believe some souls are older souls. They have had many lifetimes and experiences. And I also believe there are newer souls—people who have not had as many lifetimes yet.

We come with a purpose. Things our souls sign up for before we enter this world. I think we pick an entire life plan and some ideas for when we get off course. I believe we pick our parents, soulmates, relationships, and everything! I imagine us having a conversation with our angels, spirit guides, and God to plan all this out. We talk about what we want to bring to this lifetime that we are getting ready for. We plan what we want to do, experience, and lessons we need to learn and go through. I think you have 100 percent picked your life. But we also have free will, so we are always allowed to change course or find new directions. We all want to know our purpose, right? Wouldn't that make things so much easier?! If we just knew our plan. But that's where the whole experience of life itself is a huge part of our purpose. Remembering who we really are and what our purpose IS the experience. I think when our free will takes us off our higher path, we can always climb right back on. It's always up to us.

Now, here is the hard part to wrap our human brains around, and one of the hardest things for me to understand, to be honest. I know some of you may be reading this and thinking, I would have NEVER picked my parents. I completely understand this; some things children have to go through in their childhoods are absolutely heartbreaking. I think souls who have picked very hard childhoods are actually some of the absolute bravest souls alive. I will never truly understand this with my human brain. I myself have a lot of questions about this part, particularly because I'm incredibly sensitive to children. So, I will share what I have grown to learn and understand the best I can. But if it doesn't feel right or truthful in your own heart, that's okay. I completely understand. Take what resonates and leave the rest. You are allowed to have your own truth as well.

I think souls who signed up for these childhoods actually came to remember their purpose in a greater capacity. They came to show the truth. They came to heal generational trauma in their ancestor lineage. They came to break through and find forgiveness, even if they were deeply tormented by the heaviness of anger or the "why me?" mentality. (Rightly so). I think at any time in your life, you can break free of your heaviness. It doesn't mean you have to forget who hurt you, but *it's not you*. Your hurt is not who you are. You are a beautiful soul that was brave enough to walk the path you have come.

I don't think it will ever seem fair if children get hurt in any way, shape, or form. Mentally, physically, emotionally—none of this is okay to me. I will never understand it. But I believe when we are all up in heaven, we think, *I can do this; I will remember I am supposed to experience this to heal, turn around, and not only speak my truth but help others who have walked in the same pain.* We just forget, like so many of us do. We get trapped in energy that is not even our own. We hang onto things and experiences, believing they are who we are, when we could shift our energy and realize we hold the power to let go of anything no longer serving us. We have the energy to heal. We have the energy to move forward and help others do the same. I believe every single soul has the ability to heal, remember, pursue their purpose, and feel like they are truly alive and well. You just have to believe it, too.

Believe in yourself. Because even though I'm saying it, it's in you, not me! The more people who can remember and choose to heal, the less trauma we will have in the world. There will be fewer hurt people. More people are awakening to understand this. They are choosing to remember who they really are, no matter what they have been through or where they have come from. They are the truth seekers, the empaths, and the ones who, even as children, could see past what hurt adults were telling them. They feel connected to the truth and who they really are. They want changes in their own communities and humanity overall. They are the ones changing the world for the better. They chose the path to heal to help not only themselves, but others all around them. I love this quote by 13th-century poet Rumi, "The wound is the place where the light enters you."

Maybe sometimes we didn't pick or choose all the trauma, and it wasn't in the plan. Did someone else's path get so off course it tangled with our own? Remember, it's all connected. One of my favorite movies of all time is *Crash*. Have you seen it? I love this movie and now understand why it impacted me so long ago. It's about 12 different people and what they experience for two days in L.A. It is such a great example of how all our energy is connected and how my energy and path can somehow affect yours as well. The movie shows how every decision these people made or did not make ended up affecting each other in the most random ways. None of them knew each other, but it was all connected, and perhaps for reasons we sometimes never understand. But I do believe there is a bigger picture on the other side—we just can't see it.

I imagine us with little energetic invisible lines being divinely guided, pulled, and pushed away from different paths. Do we listen to the pulls and pushes? Or do we ignore them? I think it's our choice. I think if we are in alignment with our true and highest selves, it's impossible to miss what is there for us. We just have to be open to seeing it, experiencing it, and feeling it. When terrible things happen to people, I think our guardian angels are right there with us, weeping for us and with us. They whisper, "This is not who you are. We will get through this." I think they are begging us to listen, feel guided, and feel loved from within, no matter what our path has looked like. They are always there for us. You're always one thought away from changing your entire life, so believe in yourself. You are never alone. And deeply loved.

I also think we pick big things, like having big dreams, or maybe we choose in this lifetime we want to live a simpler life. I think we choose things we know will make our soul happy, experiences that will expand our soul, and experiences we want to live! This looks different for everyone. But every one of us knows that when we are planning this, we all think and come from a place where our soul's path is abundant and filled with love, wealth, and purpose. Abundance is here for everyone!

We didn't come to experience lack. That is our ego telling us that. It tells us we aren't good enough, things will never change, and only certain people are gifted abundance. Whatever story you are telling yourself, it is not your soul self but your ego. Your true self believes deeply in you and your ability to become abundant in *all* areas of your life, no matter what or where you came from. It's all inside of you. Remember, with God, all things are possible! Don't limit yourself. Believe in yourself, trust yourself, and take action to get yourself there.

I think our invisible, energetic lines bring us to certain relationships as well. From friendships to romantic partners, when we are really connected to who we really are, we can really start to feel the people we are meant to be around and the friends who we instantly have a connection with and feel we have known them for years!

There are some relationships where something feels a bit different! They just get you. I believe this is also all set up with our divine selves. We are meant to pay attention to those feelings and the people who we connect with on a deep level. I think soulmates can be friends, siblings, and parents, not just romantic partners. I think we have many soulmates. I think we were up in heaven with our soul family, wanting to experience this lifetime together in whatever way that we chose. Our relationships are such a big part of life's purpose. We are meant to experience life! We are meant to have connections and embrace them. The people we do life with are our best teachers. Even if they trigger you, they are expanding you. You either grow and heal from it, or you hang on to the negative aspects and energy from it. It's completely up to you. You are in control of you.

What relationships make you feel your best is up to you! I encourage you to embrace healthy relationships, though. And I think when we are really connected to our soul self, our hearts, and living and embracing our highest path, we see beautiful relationships walk into our lives. We are the energy field attracting and bringing certain things into our lives. That's why leaning into this part of who we truly are is so important—and knowing and understanding what attracts us to higher frequencies all around us.

The biggest piece of advice I would give to the younger generation and my own children would be to embrace who you really are. If you feel like you can't be yourself, that person is absolutely not an energetic match or soulmate for you. If you feel connected to your own truth, your own heart, you know your worth. You won't allow someone to treat you with anything other than respect because you respect yourself. I also think when we are living our soul's path, we are happier. We are energetically vibrating higher, and that attracts the right relationships on our path as well. Higher vibrations attract higher-vibration relationships. We might not ever understand divine timing, but you won't need to settle. You are so worthy of having a beautiful and healthy relationship. Everyone deserves this, and it is possible for everyone. Once again, we just have to believe this within ourselves.

CHAPTER 7

Heaven–Like

"*Heaven is under our feet as well as over our heads.*"
– Henry David Thoreau

First off, I want to say I am not writing from heaven right now, just in case we forget this. I'm sitting in my bedroom with my doggies. I have the window open because it's a beautiful day. The kids are at school, and I promised myself that today would be a writing day. This, in a way, has become a version of heaven on earth for me. I love writing and letting the words just come out of me. It's almost as if I feel like I'm in a trance-like state, and they just pour out. I didn't even know they were there to begin with. I feel as though I open my heart and say, "GO!" and write what comes out. It happens so effortlessly. Many people refer to this as automatic writing—something I never imagined would be possible just a few years ago. Me writing a book? No way! Not me. How would I even fill the pages? I think it's because I trust myself now. I surrendered and have shifted into my heart. I turned my lifeline on to my higher power, filled with knowledge and wisdom, just like all of you can do as well.

I know my heart wants to speak, and I believe part of my purpose in my lifetime is to share my spirituality, angel messages, and help others do the same. But I don't have all the answers. I will always be growing and learning. I just know, with the deepest part of my heart, what feels true to me now. It is what I have awakened to and have felt for myself. It's my own truth and my authentic self. It's like my whole body wants to scream, "This is true!" Not just for me, but for all of you! It's possible to connect and awaken to this part of us. All of us have the right to connect with our divine selves. It's our birthright! It's why we came here. We wanted to remember this part of us.

Let's talk about heaven. No matter your thoughts or beliefs about heaven, we can't help but wonder what it is. Where do we go when we die? What does it really look like? Do only certain people get in?

Do we get a better spot in heaven if we judge others and make them feel less than we do because we know the right way into heaven, and they don't? Should we roll our eyes in judgment because they believe something different from us? Should we start wars, only vote for certain politicians who also know the right way to heaven, and not include certain groups of humans because our direct line and ticket to heaven is better? Surely, if we do those things, God must give us a better ticket into heaven? Because if God is love, it is definitely love to show others who are right and wrong! God will be so impressed with me for getting the best seat up there that I'll get promoted in heaven.

I wonder if this actually goes through some people's minds? Because when I look out into the world, it is so easy to find judgment, anger, resentment, and pointing the finger at who's right and who's wrong. People feel superior to others because of their religious beliefs. Some also hold back from getting to know groups of people because of their religious beliefs. Wars actually start because of religious beliefs. Innocent, beautiful souls are killed because someone had a different belief from them.

People turn away family members because of the choices they make—like who they choose to love or not—even when it's their own child's truth. If that truth doesn't align with someone else's religious beliefs, fear takes over. They worry that by accepting and loving this person (which is what God truly represents), they might jeopardize their own place in heaven. As a result, they turn away their children for having different truths. Instead of seeking to understand, learn, grow, and expand—which is what our soul is meant to do—they let their ego guide them, choosing judgment over love and connection. I don't think we can believe that God is love and also believe He would not allow us into heaven if we choose to love our children and show them love, no matter the path they have taken. Remember, that is their soul. Yours is your own. You get to choose love at all times, no matter what. That is what I think God truly is. Unconditional love.

I definitely do not have all the answers—I am human, after all. But I deeply feel in my heart we all go to heaven, and we have a choice while we are on earth. Do we live in heaven on earth? Or do we live in hell? It's completely up to us; we have free will.

I believe that when it's time for us to transition to the other side, our soul is met by our team. This team includes our guardian angels who have been with us since birth, our spirit guides and loved ones who have already transitioned, and maybe even some religious figures who we have felt deeply connected to in this lifetime, such as Jesus, Buddha, Mother Mary, and others. These are just a few examples.

You can stay in heaven for as long as you want or need to before your soul wants to experience a physical life again. As I mentioned earlier, I do believe we have past lives and future lives. Many people still need *to* heal after leaving their bodies, especially if they didn't heal while on Earth.

When we return to our soul selves, we leave behind so much heaviness, trauma, and ego. We return to our truest selves. Our most divine part. We return to the *truth* of who we really are. But what we don't leave behind is our experiences and knowledge from this current lifetime. We can finally see a clearer picture of why and what we were doing here or what we are supposed to do. We connect and see that plan again, thinking, *Oh man! I forgot about that!*

I have interviewed many mediums, psychics, channels, near-death experience (NDE) stories, and spiritual teachers on my podcast called *A Well + Nourished Soul*. They all had similar stories, which is fascinating because none of them knew each other. A lot of them didn't even know my own personal story or beliefs. They all said almost the exact same things, just in different little ways—we don't just die. They believe that when our soul transitions, we are met with our team. This can look different for everyone since we all have our own teams. No one is forgotten, so everyone will be welcomed by their spirit guides, angels, maybe even a grandmother/grandfather, or past loved one. You will be welcomed with love, no matter what you have walked through or experienced in this lifetime. You are back to your soul self; it's filled with love, and so is everyone else around you. This is when you will be presented with what they have all called a "Life Review."

It's been explained a few different ways to me. Think of yourself as watching a movie of your life from childhood to adulthood. You will instantly feel happy or sad, or maybe have a moment (or a few moments) when you weren't your best human self and the pain you caused someone else. You will be watching your life experiences being played out right in front of you. Everything. Well, you may be thinking, won't that take a long time? Time is not the same on the other side, and I won't be writing about time not being linear because I'm human. I don't think I can ever wrap my mind around that. (*Ha!*) Seek quantum physics books out for that one!

I have always been fascinated by this life review. When so many spiritually gifted humans explain it, I always ask, "Why do we go through this?" And it simply is to remind you that you came here for a reason. *You* have a purpose. Your purpose is to *live* your life full of love, full of growth, full of healing, and full of experiences. Some are good, and some are bad. This is truly what we came to do. Our life review is us being able to expand and grow instantly with all the life lessons we have walked through in our current life. We feel other people's pain. We can feel our own pain. We feel others' joys, and I think we finally see the bigger picture at that moment and how it's all connected. How the whole time, we were *never* alone. We were always being nudged onto a certain path for a reason. We met certain people for a reason. We went through good and bad experiences for a reason. I also think we realize that how I treated someone else can absolutely affect them and their path, or how the decision you made led to another decision down the road. On and on, it's all related. Remember, we are all energy. Our actions, words, and thoughts are all energy. So yes, it absolutely gets all tangled up together, good and bad. This is a reminder for you that no matter what, you get to keep being tangled up or untangle your energy. *You* get to decide. You are *you*.

This also makes me circle back to what really makes life so much more meaningful in our everyday interactions. With ourselves and even with the small encounters we may have with people at a coffee shop, you never know how you're affecting others and how that is affecting you. It also makes those simplest of life's pleasures have so much more deep and powerful meanings: the baseball games, the nights out with your closest girlfriends laughing the night away, reading a new favorite book, watching a funny movie, swimming in the ocean, making a beautiful dinner, telling people you love them, and opening your home up to your loved ones. We could go on and on!

It's the littlest things that I think will impact you the most at the end of your life. Why? Because that is what living is. *Experiencing* life! We just forget this. It's so easy nowadays. We are thrown so much noise to cover up our lights, our souls, and our truths. We have piles of bills and endless distractions online, and we can feel like we will never leave a certain situation: anxiety, depression, addiction, war, or abuse. We could go on and on, inserting so much heaviness. I feel like that is the darkness trying to distract our light. We have to remember our lights can get covered, but they can never be blown out. We are all souls. Our lights and energetic strings to God or source can't be cut off with energetic scissors by anyone outside of us. They can be dimmed, confused, or conflicted by outside sources—but never cut off.

At any time in your life, you have the power to get yourself on the right path. You have the control to have your soul start to lead you back to the path that you were created for. When you watch your life review, other people are not making the calls and the shots. The life review is not about someone making the decisions for you or not. It's about *your* life. *Your* soul. Maybe someone else did and is still making life decisions for you. Or you are living your life in fear because you want to feel worthy of whoever it is. Or living in fear of trying new things or experiences because you are afraid of what others will think or say.

Let me tell you, friends, out of the hundreds of conversations I have had with others and my own angels, this life is for you and *your* soul. You will not be sitting there at that moment watching your "Life Review" and a parent, in-law, friend, religious leader, partner, or teacher comes in and starts telling you what you should or should not have done. Nope. It's just you and your own energy. Your own points of view. Your own path. You will be watching the dreams you did or did not create. The connections you did or did not make. The time you did or did not invest in yourself and your family. I'm sure that when we take time to appreciate the simplest moments and witness the connections with our loved ones, our hearts will be so full of love that they feel ready to burst. I don't think you get rewarded for working your life away—whoever gets the most money wins. I don't think if you have lived your life with a fear of not getting into heaven, so you've been judgmental about others, not experienced what you really want to experience, and so on, you get rewarded. I think in those moments, we are either filled with regret or love. Maybe a bit of both since we have let go of the ego at that point. It is your life you are going to be watching. So, what kind of movie are you going to watch when your time comes?

CHAPTER 8

Is There Such a Thing as Bad Souls?

"We are spiritual beings immersed in a human experience."
– Dr. Wayne Dyer

If we are *all* going to heaven and going back to where we came from after this life, what happens to people who were evil in their lifetime? Do people who abuse children get punished, please? (My soul feels crushed knowing children are abused in any way, and I can't stand to think people just get away with this.) There are also lots of different ways evil plays out all over the world. Wars, worldwide leaders who are evil themselves, corruption, cover-ups, murders, drugs, child abuse, human trafficking; I mean, we can go on and on, as we all know there is evil here. What happens to all the evil people after their human life is done?

Since I don't really believe God sends you to hell to punish you for eternity, I had to sit with this and really dig deep into what feels true in my heart about all this. I had to know something happened to these souls. They can't just get away with all their evil on earth! Or is that my ego talking? I'm not sure we will ever truly know or understand until it's our time to transition, but I will share what I feel is true in my heart. In Helen Schucman's book, *A Course in Miracles*, this quote is so powerful, "Hell is only what the ego has made of the present."[1]

What does that mean? Well, I believe that we have a choice while we are here. I feel like Earth is hell if you *choose* to live in that energetic field while you are here. It's your choice. Do you live in heaven on earth? Or do you live in hell? With lower frequencies, evil prevails, almost as if these people really have left their souls. They run their life from their ego and only their ego. Their physical bodies are here, but their souls are deeply forgotten about. Disconnected from God and the truth of who they really are.

We can see examples all over the world where we see darkness or evil being played out. Or maybe you've walked into a certain place or city and just don't have a great feeling. Sometimes our inner knowing gives us a feeling we can't quite explain—something just feels off. We can see people at times that just look like their "lights" seem off. Something seems like it's missing. Addiction can be an example of someone completely leaving their body. Meaning their soul may not be in their body. But their body is still here, just walking around. They are lost in addiction and living on the streets, or surviving day to day in their own houses, and we see this played out in so many ways all over our world. But wow, the addiction problem is bad in the U.S. And to me, it's heartbreaking. We all must also remember addiction does not discriminate. I feel so strongly about this, as I have seen this in my own family. This circles back to humans helping other humans *be* human. We have no idea what people have walked through.

I don't think it's just an addiction that is hell. I think hell can be played out in many different ways or scenarios. I think hell can be as simple as people pretending they are living a great life to the outside world when, behind closed doors, they are filled with choices fueled by

---

1. Helen Schucman, *A Course in Miracles* (Mill Valley, CA: Foundation for Inner Peace, 1976), T-15.I7:2.

ego or darkness and completely disconnected from their lights from within. If their soul is covered by darkness, they can't feel good from within. It's not possible. I think if you are not living in truth, you are living in fear. So, if you are allowing darkness to cover your light, it's not authentic. In some way or form, you are living in fear. Fear of getting caught? Fear of losing control? Fear of lacking something? If you aren't living with yourself, covered in truth, which is light, you know you're hiding something. No matter what you tell yourself, this creates fear. Are you still with me? Ha-ha. A simpler way to look at it is that truth = light. If you aren't living in truth, you aren't living in light. John 14:6 says, *"The holy spirit is the spirit of truth."*

Let me explain more. I also think it's okay to believe whatever you want to about this subject because you aren't in charge of another soul and what happens to them after they leave their physical bodies. No matter what your beliefs are, God is the only one in charge of all our souls. So the good news is that if you don't believe in any of what I'm saying, I'm not in charge of your soul! Phew. If we believe God is pure love, how could we also believe He sends souls to hell to burn for eternity when He Himself created these souls from love? And I'm talking about love that is limitless, powerful beyond our wildest imagination, and full of everything besides anger and judgment. It is an unconditional love. Would it be hypocritical of us to believe that God's love is limitless, yet He judges us and wants to punish us?

Corinthians 13:4 defines love this way: *"Love is patient, love is kind. It does not envy, it does not boast, it is not proud. It does not dishonor others, it is not self-seeking, it is not easily angered, it keeps no record of wrongs."*

Some scriptures point out that love keeps no records of wrongdoing, but other parts say there is sin. If love keeps no records of wrongs, which would be sinning? Which one is it? There are also religions that believe as long as you sin, but then repent, you are okay. God will forgive you. So don't worry about all that abuse you covered up with hundreds of children's souls you deeply impacted in such a negative way. As long as you told God you sinned and asked for forgiveness, you are cleared.

(Sigh. That one really gets to me) How can you say you love God yet turn the other way if a child is being abused? Or worse, help cover this up in any way, shape, or form. I wanted to know this first thing when I awakened. I reached out to some of the most gifted mediums and spiritual teachers seeking this answer. Because it was a hard part for me to understand. Does God keep a record of this stuff, or does He not?

I wholeheartedly believe that not living in truth/light would be darkness. So, continually lying to yourself and others would be living in fear because you are lying to yourself in some way, shape, or form. And fear does not come from the light. So my guess is, if you are living this life, truth in some way, shape, or form, will be making its way to you at some time in your life. Light will always cover the darkness. We are seeing a lot of darkness come to light all over the world right now. I deeply believe we will continue to do so over the next few years. More and more truth is coming to light.

When it's our time to transition, we are then presented with our life review and our team. Like I mentioned previously. It is at that moment that you will have to review a lifetime in which you may have caused hurt to others in any way, shape, or form. You may have thought you were going to get away with it, but I think this will be your time when it all comes back to you. You will feel all the pain you caused others. You will watch, with your angels, your spirit guides, your team, all the suffering you brought to the world. But you won't be just watching; your soul will be deeply feeling this suffering itself.

We have to remember our divine self—our soul self—leaves the ego and the human brain behind. We aren't thinking, nor are the angels, from a human perspective. Everyone thinks and really feels from their divine self. Their soul self. There is no more anger, resentment, judgment, or confusion. It's pure love. We know exactly what we have done in those moments. And we feel them deeply. The good, the bad, and the very ugly. I can't imagine what souls feel who created a lot of evil while living on earth. My guess is it's unimaginable.

I have also asked so many mediums this question and am fascinated by what they have to say. Since they have provided thousands and thousands of readings for people who have already transitioned, I am fascinated and deeply interested in their answers. What comes after that life review? What do the past loved ones who come through in your readings have to say about all this? I've asked many, have read so many books on this, and have asked the angels myself, and this is what I have learned.

Even though we return to our soul selves after we die and leave behind our ego, we can still feel emotion, especially from our earthly lifetime(s). Mediums say the number one emotion people feel is love. The next one is regret. Maybe it's a father who never took the time to be emotionally invested in his family or was never there in the first place. When he returns to his soul self, he instantly remembers who he really is and what his purpose was in his lifetime. He is instantly washed away from the heaviness, maybe even his own trauma from his childhood and lifetime. He is instantly returned to his soul being and filled with God's love but also regret. He can see/feel/hear how his life then impacted those around him. Generational trauma enters the chat. He then wants nothing more than to help or guide his family, which he did or maybe did not do while on Earth. He wants nothing more than to fill that child (who is now an adult) with the love they never got from him. Why? Because He can see clearly at that point.

We are lifted from the darkness of our choices and the states of frequency we chose to live or not live in. We are lifted from our trauma and returned to the light. We begin to see from a new perspective, realizing how much meaning and purpose our life held. Our purpose was not just about ourselves but also about the impact we had on everyone around us. I feel like the spirits of our loved ones are waving their magic wands every day so that all of us living humans can understand this. They send us signs and signals, and try to connect with all of us. They want all of us to know you will have regrets if you choose to live your life in darkness. If you don't find healing while living, you will see and feel what trauma you have left behind you that is still walking on earth.

So much darkness can come from trauma as a child. Souls are not born evil. It's not possible. If we believe in a God who is pure love, we cannot also believe that He created evil souls. I think there is darkness here (hell on earth) that can cover our lights of love from within all of us. It tries to pull you down. I think this can stem from deep childhood trauma, low frequencies, low self-worth, addiction, generational trauma, and whether we choose to heal or not. But God did not create evil. We humans did. We are all energy. Everything is energy. Energy vibrates at either a high frequency or low frequency, according to quantum physics. So, if we vibrate at a low frequency, we attract low frequencies all around us and in our energetic field.

But here is the good news: No matter what we have been through in our life, we have the choice to heal. We have the choice to step out of darkness and return to our own very powerful lights. We have the choice not to live life in a victim mentality at any time in our lifetime. No matter what you have walked through, you can heal and return to the bright light you were created to be and created from. That does not mean it will be easy. It will always be work to heal. But I believe anyone has the capability to do so. I don't want you to regret it on the other side. What do you need to heal from? How can you feel more connected to your true divine self while walking on this earth? That's choosing to live in heaven on earth. And then you get to start watching the magic happen!

Many mediums have also talked about souls who have really walked in darkness while on earth and may need time to really heal in heaven. Some have explained it as almost like a soul hospital. Your soul will need a lot of healing. These souls will need time away before they return to loved ones, heaven itself, and the party on the other side! So maybe that is some form of "hell," to be honest. I feel like I envision it as darker lights returning to their bright and beautiful color. It reminds me of the kids' movie *Trolls*. Branch does not live in color, but as Poppy starts to remind him of his true self, his color returns, and he starts singing because that's who he really was and what he loved to do. I think so many of us forget about the music we carry inside of us. We lose our color. And we don't let the music out. We get stuck, trapped, confused, and *poof*, so much life goes by us.

I also believe souls won't be returned to earth for a very long time if they have major healing to do from their time on earth and lived in so much darkness. Until they are fully restored and healed, they will then have to learn a lot in heaven. There are some phenomenal teachers up there who I know are helping. Can you imagine taking a class from Jesus? Buddha? How fascinating! I think that a lot of the souls that get mixed up with darkness while here on earth may be newer souls. They have easily forgotten who they really are and where they come from. I think it's easier for newer souls to have a harder time on earth. So, when they return home and they see the bigger picture, they have some learning and healing to do.

No matter our soul's age, we are all continuing to learn. We are constantly learning, growing, expanding, searching for information, and helping others. So, the souls who get covered with darkness while they are on Earth may have some lessons they will then have to come back to Earth to experience. In simple terms, it's kinda like Karma. I think they are kept in a place where they really have to work on some things, and then it's their choice when they come back to earth about what lessons they will have to go through. I don't think God sends them as a punishment. I think our souls, when they return to pure love and light, want to experience more lessons. They want to help others. When we really grasp and are in full remembrance of who we really are and what we were supposed to do, I think we can regret our choices at times in our lives. And I believe that as our souls learn, heal, and grow, we then choose a new lifetime. And if we were living on earth and made terrible and evil choices in our last lifetime, I think our soul actually will choose hard lessons for us from the opposite perspective in their next lifetime. What do you think? What feels true to your own heart? It's okay to feel differently on this. I would love to hear your own perspectives!

Here are some more examples of regrets I have heard from the other side, from the mediums themselves, and through my own angel readings. I have heard so much regret about people living their lives in fear of other people's opinions. They wished they had pursued the dream they always wanted, moved to the place they longed to live, connected more with friends, taken up hobbies they were too nervous to try, written the book, taken a vacation, and worked less. The most common regret I hear is not being able to show love like they wanted to. Maybe that was hard for them to do for whatever reason in this lifetime, but when they see clearly, and they are returned to that love, that's all they want to give. In one way or another, much of the regret is simply about not fully *living* life itself.

When we are constantly trying to win someone's approval or even our own approval, are we really living life? And whose approval are we seeking so desperately? There hasn't been one time I have not heard loved ones say how unbelievably proud they are of so-and-so when they are connecting. No matter if they said that here in this lifetime or not, they can see all that clearly on the other side and feel it deeply. They know how hard life can be. They understand fully what we all have to go through. I feel like they are shaking us all awake to say, "LIVE YOUR LIFE! LOVE YOUR LIFE!" They want us to experience our life in all the ways of love by slowing down, really being present, and fully taking in how beautiful life truly is. These are the small things of our day-to-day hustle.

From small moments and connections with our children—such as snuggles, kisses, family meals, and laughter—to the world's beauty, romance, the dreams in our hearts, and freedom, they remind us that it's all truly there. They all have a lot to say, a lot of things they can teach and help us with, and help heal our generational trauma as well. They are here for us with love, whether we know that in this lifetime or not.

I also want to say that I'm writing about this and thinking about all of it from an adult perspective. We are reading this in our adult lives. Still, I can't help but think about the children who live in abusive situations every single day—my heart can't comprehend it. It makes me wish there were some form of punishment. I'm being honest. No matter how spiritual I am, this subject is the absolute hardest for me to understand and write about. My ego won't let go. I want people who harm children to face consequences.

Children in those situations are not creating that experience. They are not attracting low frequencies to them. They have no choice. Children are vulnerable—they don't have the options that we, as adults, do. They need help. They need us, collectively, to protect them. I want to make that clear because, as I wrote this chapter, I kept circling back to this.

This is where I personally struggle with spirituality, religion, and beliefs in general. What should I believe? Why is there so much suffering? I think it's easier for us to simply assume that these people go to hell —the end, goodbye. And honestly, I agree with you. But everything I have awakened to understand in my own heart leads me back to what I've been writing about all along.

I want to say this: collectively, we need to do better for our children. The entire world needs to heal their hearts, their generational trauma, their addiction, their mental health, their limiting beliefs, their endless search outside of them, the crippling anxiety, the superiority because of religion or routes to God, the greed, the insert whatever story it is you tell yourself.

WE HAVE TO DO BETTER FOR THE CHILDREN OF THIS WORLD. No child deserves to be raised in an abusive, neglectful, or traumatic environment. NONE. The only way we can change this collectively is if we wake up to the truest parts of who we are within our own hearts. If we start remembering we have the ability to help or heal anyone, we start understanding we are all connected. We can help the children in our own communities. We can help the children who need us. We can even help their parents. Once we truly understand how to support one another in our shared humanity—like I mentioned earlier—we can transform this world into a place where children no longer have to endure suffering.

We won't have to ask what happens to these souls, because there will no longer be souls covered in darkness. I know this may seem impossible, because not everyone will choose to heal in this lifetime. But it only takes you... and you... and you... and so on—to truly make a difference. To end the cycles. To break free. To help others.

I believe this with my entire heart.

Don't look the other way when you see a child in need or sense that something is wrong. Pray for them, cover them in your light and love, and show them what is possible. Help them!

On the medical side of all this, I wish we could start asking different questions. I don't think there are bad souls, but I do think there are "bad" brains. I do know there is research on this, and doctors are pouring their hearts and purpose into this research. And I'm very thankful for them.

In my personal opinion, I think everyone should be able to get brain scans when they need help with mental health in any capacity. It does seem crazy to me that most psychologists do not even look at the brain itself. I'm no expert in any way, but that seems like it should be just the first step, right? Step 1: Get a brain scan, then go on with treatment from there. Maybe I'm wrong, but as a curious person—someone who sees things differently from the systems we have in place—this makes sense to me. Mental health issues are everywhere, affecting people of all ages. Especially in our country, can we at least start trying?

Imagine teens who are deeply troubled seeking medical attention for mental health concerns—only to be shown scans of their brain. Imagine if they were taught how their brain did or did not develop differently due to trauma or external experiences. This could be incredibly helpful. What if they truly understood this instead of constantly being told a different story about who they are and what medication they need? What if we focused on improving their brain health?

Whether it's children, teens, young adults, or older adults, I feel like we are missing something—something that could be profoundly beneficial to our overall well-being. We just need to start looking at the systems we have in place differently. (Once again.)

Sometimes, it seems so simple. Why can't we just do these things? Why can't doctors learn more about brain imaging and mapping—and make it easy and accessible for families to have it done routinely? (I know this isn't just doctors' fault, I really do.) Can you imagine if brain scans were part of our children's yearly wellness check? To see how their brain is developing?

As I mentioned earlier, I don't believe there are bad souls, but I do believe there are "bad" brains. Not inherently bad brains, but brains that have developed differently for reasons beyond an individual's control.

I keep imagining these future wellness centers in my mind. Yes, I repeat—*in my imagination.* This may seem crazy to some, but let's be creative together for a minute. It would be incredible to develop these for real. Imagine this: **Soul Wellness Centers.**

First, you walk into the doctor's office, and they scan your brain. Next, you head to get your energetic body scanned. I imagine holding onto something—like one of those body scanners—and then, right in front of us, through a mirror or some kind of display, we can actually *see* all the energy we are—colors, movement, everything. We can pinpoint where energy is getting stuck or tangled and what needs our focus. Then, they run full blood work, hormone testing—everything. No more bouncing between ten different doctors; it's all done here, in one place. Afterward, you're sent to an energy healer to balance your energetic body based on your scan from that day.

Next, a doctor comes in to review your brain imaging. They explain what's happening in your mind and discuss which supplements or practices can optimize your brain health and overall well-being. They actually *listen*—deeply and intently—to your thoughts, emotions, and concerns. They talk about your nutrition, movement plan, and energy levels, tailoring recommendations based on your brain and energetic footprint scan. Then comes sound healing. A session designed to raise your frequency and presence from within—to enhance your joy, happiness, and overall health.

This center is filled with healers, doctors of all specialties, nutritionists, and intuitives, all working together. You get your blood results back and guess what? You don't need medication—because you are living your best life! You're healthy, happy, joyful, and fully aligned with your true self. You're caring for your body, mind, and spirit in ways that genuinely nourish you.

And now... *back to reality.* Your bill? $50,000. Insurance? Doesn't cover it. *Sigh.* Come on, people at the top—let's start funding research and doing something different. We desperately need it! *Hint, hint to those in power: heal your own hearts first.*

In all seriousness, things that we *do* know are that good and bad experiences can rewire our brains differently. It's a process called neuroplasticity. That is scientifically proven. But I personally believe that our hearts (our spirits) have a lot to do with all of this as well. This brings us to the very powerful question of: "Are there bad souls?" I don't think there are. I think lights can be covered by darkness, dimmed, and it rewires our brain and signals it to work differently. I also understand our brains can be damaged or develop differently for many different reasons. Not just childhood trauma.

What it really comes down to is the powerful connection between our heart and mind—perhaps the most powerful connection there is. Our souls are unbelievably strong, our light holds the truth of who we are, and within us exists an immense amount of magic and love. But when certain experiences disconnect us from our hearts—when our hearts are deeply wounded, confused, or struggling to make sense of pain—our brains, our human selves, adapt. They rewire and program themselves differently in an attempt to cope. I believe it's all connected.

When our spirit struggles to co-mingle with our physical body, we begin to shut it down, preventing ourselves from fully aligning with who we truly are. In response, our brain rewires itself the best it can based on the experiences—or lack of experiences—it is having. But what if we collectively shifted our perspective? What if we asked different questions—about brain health, trauma, nutrition, experiences, love, and our spirit?

I have personally witnessed how reaching deep within ourselves—helping people heal their souls and hearts—directly improves their overall well-being. It helps their brain. It helps their thoughts. I would love to see what a brain scan would show before and after an angel reading. It would be fascinating. Dr. Amen, are you out there? Let's make this happen. (*Haha!*)

I believe love can clear a lot of things out of our systems. Love can clear the darkness that so many of us get trapped in and can't seem to let go of. The cycles, the pattern, the stories we tell ourselves. What we really need is *Love*. Love for ourselves. Love for each other. Self-worth. And sometimes, no matter how much we consciously want to change things, it's that darn subconscious that stores the programming and our limiting beliefs. The trauma and our experiences we have hung onto since our childhood. The voices of people telling us who we are or who we are not.

Remember, we are all different! And no matter what you have walked through, you have the power to heal yourself. I believe it's possible for all of us. I feel like there is a deep calling within the collective to truly go within. To be more curious about all this. To put more research into all of this. To be more curious about this connection of the mind and heart specifically. To our energetic bodies. Awaken to this part of who you are and heal the parts of you that need to be let go of.

We are able to rewire our brains at any age through new experiences and focused effort—through healing ourselves. And let me remind you, healing does take work, but our bodies are simply amazing. Anything is possible.

Now, more than ever, this is important because when we heal, we can turn around and create bright paths for our children to step into, rather than dark ones. They deserve this. They deserve to have that mind-heart connection wide open—and to keep it open! They deserve to be led by parents who love themselves and show love to their children.

Children deserve to shine their light brightly. It's who they truly are.

I want to end this chapter with a prayer for the children of the world; I intuitively feel like I'm being guided to bring up children over and over in this book. Our children need us. In many different ways, all over the world. It all starts with us. Healing ourselves.

> *God, I'm praying to you to cover the children of this world in your light. Help them understand and know how much love is within them. Help them remember who they really are and how much power and love resides within them no matter what circumstances*

they are currently living in. Shine light over them and cover them with love and safety. Lead them to true love and guidance, their earth angels. Protect our children of this world, remove darkness from their hearts, and let them see the truth of who they are. I pray the angels are with them and keep them comfortable in times they are needing it. Help the world see and understand that children are one of the most sacred gifts we have on this planet. Help the world see that we have the ability to change this planet for the better with your help, with your guidance. Help us all protect our children. All children. In your love, Amen.

CHAPTER 9

Spiritual Gifts

"Now there are varieties of gifts, but the same Spirit; and there are varieties of service, but the same Lord; and there are varieties of activities, but it is the same God who empowers them all in everyone."
– 1 Corinthians 12:4–6

Spiritual Gifts—one of my favorite topics to talk about these days. Do I believe in spiritual gifts? Wholeheartedly. And it's a huge reason I'm writing this book in the first place. Everything I have already talked about is really opening up to this part of you. I believe we all have spiritual gifts. Every single one of us. It's our divine right to be open to our gifts, but it's your choice if you fear this part of you or not. Embracing who you truly are!

I believe we all have spiritual gifts and that they look different for all of us. I believe some people have an easier connection to their gifts and that it is harder for others. This could have to do with soul ages, lessons, and what you chose to experience in this lifetime. But no matter what, you have spiritual gifts as well!

Intuition is such a trendy word these days, but it's a great example of our divine self. It's who we really are, and I think when we tap into our intuition, we tap into our spiritual gifts. We are tapping into the beautiful magic God has gifted inside of us.

I know spiritual gifts can be scary for some. If we use different words or terminology surrounding this topic, it can trigger fear in some people's programming, thinking that spiritual gifts are something to be feared, bad, or wrong. And that's what I want to talk about in this chapter. Where does this fear truly come from? Let's put our open-minded hats on for this chapter.

I believe our spiritual gifts come straight from God Himself/Herself. So why would it be something we should fear? I feel like if you read scripture in any world religion, everything is through a lens of spiritual gifts. The entire New Testament is written from a perspective of people not physically seeing Jesus but "spiritually" connecting to Him and His spirit. Why are we so open to all of this yet question or think people who do have spiritual gifts are strange or weird? Or scary? Or we don't believe in them at all and label them as crazy.

I believe this is a time when people around us are increasingly opening up to this part of themselves. They are trusting themselves and their intuition more and experiencing more spiritual moments in general. It's truly beautiful to see, and it will only serve to elevate our collective consciousness higher and higher. They are less afraid to talk about their experiences or deep, "inner knowing" and are using their God-given gifts to help not only validate and heal themselves but also help others as well.

I've used the words medium, psychic, and NDE already in this book. These are words that, at a certain time, I would have worried that I was doing something wrong to be curious about their spiritual gifts. That I would be told it was bad. Something that God would not like and punish me for. But I really want to analyze this for a second.

We already know that I think God is unconditional love. I don't think He punishes us or wants us to live in fear. I think that He, more than ever, wants us to connect with our gifts that come straight from

Him. I believe that there are mistranslations around this subject, and people also want our power to be disconnected at certain times. And throughout history. So they can feel as though they are the ones with the power themselves. If everyone was connected to their "superpowers," then there would be fewer people to control in general.

I wanted to share this experience because I want to paint a picture of curiosity from within your own heart. Why do you think God would want to keep us separate from the other side, which holds so much love and truth? Why do we think it would be bad to go and talk to someone with spiritual gifts when we are in the darkest time in our lives or maybe even grieving someone? When this person could bring so much love and light to us and heal our hearts in a way that would only be possible with this type of spiritual connection. One full of love and truth.

I don't think God wants us to feel separate from our gifts or fear this part of us or others. I really don't. I think that was man-made, not God-made. I think Jesus was one of the most spiritual beings to ever walk the earth and really tried to show us what was possible with God. He wanted to show what was possible while we are here on earth. Some people go through the most unimaginable loss of loved ones while here; why do we think God would want to keep us separate from them and their love? Their messages or their signs would make a profound impact to hear from on our hearts while still living here on earth.

Now, with that said, I do think that just like there are bad doctors, lawyers, teachers, priests, pastors, etc., there can be bad people with spiritual gifts as well. I absolutely believe that. But that should not keep us from exploring our own truths. And the truths of others. That should not keep us in the fear bubble of being curious about people's gifts! And, more importantly, our own gifts. There are BEAUTIFUL healers out there who bring through the most beautiful, life-changing messages for anyone who needs their gifts. This can be life-changing for so many of us. Hearing messages that are just for you from your divine team can be one of the most healing experiences. Knowing you are not alone. That you are surrounded by love. Validated on a soul level. This can absolutely be life-changing. I have seen it myself! (Even my own energy healing session was life-changing!)

So many of us go through life feeling so disconnected from our own inner truths. We feel so alone at times. Even if you go to church or think of yourself as very religious, that does not mean you truly are connected to the truth of who you are. It does not mean you are living from your heart. That goes the same for extreme spirituality and ego. It does not mean you're authentically connected to you. Because let me tell you I see a lot of "spiritual ego" out there. Maybe you aren't allowing yourself to feel your true connection to your own heart. Maybe there are still weeds covering your light. It is work to have to dig deep within. And some of us just do not want to work on it.

It's easier to keep it closed off. Maybe there's too much pain there, too much change, and we become afraid of that part of ourselves. We become afraid of our own power—our truth. At times, it feels easier to mask the authenticity of our spirit, to hold on to beliefs that have kept us comfortable for so long, resisting any change or new perspective. I understand.

You are allowed to feel however you want about all of this. I'm just here to cheer you and your authentic self on—no matter what.

But I also want you to know that knowing that you have a team of angels, spirit guides, and loved ones on the other side cheering you on and sending you love, messages, and ideas can feel incredibly healing. I feel like God wants you to connect to your team. He wants you to feel the incredible divine wisdom and love from within your own heart. He does not want you to feel separate from this or fear this part of you. I believe it's your divine birthright.

This goes back to me saying we are spiritual beings having a physical experience. Not the other way around. If we are spiritual beings, that's who we truly are before we come to this life, and when we leave, why should we be taught to fear this part of who we truly are? I feel like we can't even comprehend how much power we hold from within our own hearts. How much truth and wisdom lies within us. Are we afraid of our own power?

I think before we come into this lifetime, we are up in heaven, thinking we won't forget this time. We won't be disconnected from it. I feel like we all come in thinking we can do this. We can remember who we really are. How powerful we are, how much love we really are, how much love is around us, and so on. But then we get programmed and disconnected from our truth. We forget. It happens to most of us. It's a part of the Earth experience. We come to remember who we really are. I think it's a big part of our life purpose. It's just, are we brave enough to remember? We are vessels. You have the gifts so that you can help not only yourself but others. That will look different for all of us. It's supposed to! You are uniquely you, and no one on earth can do what you do precisely the way you do it. I encourage you to be truly open to this part of you. It is beautiful and full of unconditional love.

And I know I wrote about this previously, but there are SO many children with beautiful spiritual gifts on Earth right now. My personal belief is that they are the ones truly shifting the planet's frequency—just by existing in their own high vibration.

I feel like so many of these incredible souls, who are deeply sensitive to energy, are being diagnosed with various mental health disorders and labeled at a very young age. Everywhere I go, I see sensitive children, and anxiety seems to be affecting them at younger and younger ages. I just want to wrap my arms around all of them and tell them there is nothing wrong with them. I want them to feel empowered, loved, and worthy—from within.

I'm certainly not a doctor or psychologist, but I am a curious soul who loves asking questions. What if we started looking at this differently—collectively? What if, instead of labeling, we asked questions like: Could my child be sensitive to energy? To their environment? To other people's emotions? To certain foods? Are they an empath? What if we introduced them to prayer, meditation, energy healing, and sound healing? What if we offered classes that taught them how to ground their energetic bodies, how to use their eye of the heart, and how to truly listen to what they are sensing, hearing, and connecting with energetically? What if we created spaces where they felt safe, seen, and understood—where they could embrace who they really are and recognize their own power?

Imagine teaching them how much love exists within them, helping them connect with their angels, and showing them how to protect their own energy. I could go on and on. I mean, we could at least try, couldn't we? I truly hope more research goes into this in the future—but in my heart, I believe it will.

There is a great podcast out now called *The Telepathy Tapes* by Ky Dickens. If you have not yet listened, run and listen to it after you read this book. It's fascinating. It's about nonverbal autistic children who have very powerful spiritual gifts. They are kids who are telepathic and know so much about the world, people, and love. Doctors have done case studies on this, and it leaves us with undeniable evidence. I encourage everyone to listen, no matter your viewpoint.

Either way, if you believe it or not, it's nonetheless interesting. These children are beautiful souls, here to help raise the frequency and consciousness of this planet. They are here to teach us, to show us new ways of being, and they are filled with love and life from within. I truly believe we have so much to learn from them—all children, in general.

I just think we need to rethink how we structure the systems and environments we create for them in the first place. I don't have all the answers—I really don't. This isn't my area of expertise. But I do know that many of us can *feel* that something needs to change. The societal expectations we place on children don't seem to be working. The noise, the pressure—it's creeping in again. And it feels *heavy*.

The thing is, they can feel it too.

It's creating more depression, anxiety, burnout, and disconnection from the truth of who they really are. At the very least, I encourage all of us to start thinking about this differently. From teachers to coaches, parents to daycare providers, nannies to grandparents—anyone working with children—I urge you to love yourself first. Be connected to yourself. Be sensitive, encouraging, aware, and empowering to these souls—to all children. They need you. They need your bright light.

And here's my message to the world: If working with children isn't your gift, go find what *is*. Don't just be around children to *make money* or to *control* the baseball team. Go live in your purpose. Shine your light in the gifts that are uniquely yours—because we all have them. But dimming a child's light should never be an option.

Let those who truly have a calling to work with children be the ones to guide them. I have also seen incredible teachers and coaches making a profound impact—not just on my own children, but on so many others. I always tell these people that I *see* them, that I *feel* their purpose, because it's undeniable.

Working with children is a gift. If you believe it's yours, then shine brightly—so children can feel that light when they are around you. That is exactly what they need. Heart.

I'm going to be talking more about my own spiritual gifts as you read on. This is a quick warning. (*Haha!*) But I do want to mention this here. No matter what your religion or spiritual beliefs are, I want to bring up a divine being who is amazing with helping anyone whose purpose is working with children. Mother Mary.

She is someone who is great to call in if you are working with children and/or parenting children. Or maybe you're in need of mothering yourself. She is full of love, grace, compassion and light. Also reminding us that we should mother and give grace to ourselves. We are so quick to jump to guilt and shame when it comes to parenting. She truly is great in reminding us that once we let that go, give ourselves grace, we can learn and move forward.

We can always do better. When I see her around certain people—and I definitely do—I know they usually have a gift for working with children in some capacity. Or perhaps, in the future, they will bring something to light that helps children in a meaningful way. It's always beautiful to witness. She is full of love, and she is there to help whoever needs her.

I also see her around many mothers who may be struggling—feeling drained, disconnected, burned out, and in need of motherly love themselves. Always feel free to call on her. She is here to offer love and strength to anyone who needs it.

I'd like to share one of my Mother Mary stories with you all. I have many, but this one feels especially important to tell.

I was at baseball practice with my son one evening a couple of years ago, running around trying to keep my littlest one entertained—which really just meant trying to make it through practice. Like I mentioned earlier, we are usually *beautiful chaos* in some way, shape, or form wherever we go. By this point, we were all exhausted, just surviving the hour.

Since it was the beginning of the season, I was meeting some of the other parents for the first time. My energy shifted toward one mom in particular. At first, I wasn't sure why. She didn't seem as open as some of the other moms—she looked stressed and didn't seem interested in small talk. That never bothers me. We're all tired at this point in the day, and everyone has their own things going on. I completely get it. Sometimes, *I* am that mom. But I kept feeling drawn to her energy, and that's when I suddenly felt Mother Mary's presence. I felt her so strongly in my heart chakra, and to this day, I always feel her in my heart. I've always felt connected to her, but this moment was something I can't explain. My heart became so full of love that I started to tear up. It was *powerful.*

And yes, *this* was another moment when I questioned whether I was going insane—*Ha!* But I trusted it. It was far too powerful to ignore. I felt Mother Mary so strongly, and I knew—with every ounce of me, every cell in my body—that it was her. Her own heart. Her own energy. Then I heard her say to me. (It wasn't an actual voice outside of me—it was more of a strong knowing, my inner voice.) *"Pray for this mother. She needs your love, my love, and strength. She needs your prayers."* So I did just that. Instantly, I prayed for her. I asked God to cover her in light and love, to give her strength, and to send her extra love. I asked Mother Mary herself to be with her and help her. I whispered this prayer to myself, then went back to chasing my littlest one around the field and trying to survive the practice. But even as I did, my energy kept being drawn back to this mom.

I want to share something important: when I prayed for her, I didn't just say the words. I felt it in my heart. I sent her deep love. I felt God over both of us in that moment. And I felt Mother Mary. No one had any idea that this was happening. To anyone watching, I was just another mom on the sidelines—cheering on my son and playing with my daughter. And that's the beauty of it.

No one has to know when you send love or prayers to someone. If your heart tells you to do so, listen. Just listen to that voice within—the one urging you to reach out, to help, to love. It's the truest part of who you are. Some call it our higher self. Some call it the Holy Spirit. Some simply call it God. Whatever name you give it, it's the purest, most loving part of you—if you're willing to be open to it.

After practice that evening, that mom walked up to me. She hesitated for a moment before asking, "Can I share something with you?"

I smiled and said, "Absolutely!" But inside, my mind was racing. *Oh my goodness, what is going on? Did she notice I was praying for her?*

She started by saying, "Don't think I'm crazy, and I know I'm oversharing…" Little did she know, I had been thinking over and over that *I* was the crazy one that evening. Then she continued, sharing something that left me speechless.

She told me that this team was going to be hard for her to be on. She opened up and revealed that she had lost a son a few years prior—and his name was the exact same as my son's. Seeing that name on the roster, hearing it called out all evening, and watching a boy full of life running around and playing baseball—it hit her hard. Of course, she wasn't in the mood for small talk. Of course, she was just trying to hold it all together. Of course, her motherly heart was desperately in need of strength and love.

I'm pretty sure I teared up in that exact moment. I looked at her, wanting so badly to tell her what had happened during practice. To tell her about Mother Mary. About the prayer. About the overwhelming love surrounding her. To tell her that she was not alone and that her son was *still* with her. But I wasn't brave enough. A part of me will always regret that. Instead, I simply told her how incredibly grateful I was that she shared her story with me. What she didn't know was how deeply grateful *I* was.

As I walked to my car, I fought to hold it together. But once I got in,

I let the tears fall. I cried for a mother who had lost her son. I cried for the miracle that I *knew* had taken place—that Mother Mary had come to me, telling me to pray for her. And I cried because I knew, without a doubt, that her son was there with us too. Maybe *he* was the one connecting it all together.

The validation of what had happened during that practice left me speechless. In that moment, I made a promise to God: I would always listen. I would always trust. I would always be open to sharing love with others who needed His messages. However they came through me, I wanted to help. Even if it meant looking "crazy," I didn't care—I wanted to help.

There are so many hurting people all around us. But if we stay open to the miracles within us, we can become the vessels of light that each other truly needs. Because sometimes, just being human is hard—and we don't have to go through it alone.

I encourage you to be open to your own spiritual gifts. Your own truth. The real you. It really does open you up to a world of possibilities, strength and a profound love for yourself and humanity. We can use our gifts in different ways just in our everyday life. I feel like there are many gifted musicians, artists, athletes, authors, speakers, doctors, teachers, entrepreneurs who are definitely connected to this part of them. They are bringing through a higher version of themselves. I believe it's possible for all of us to do even though we all have different gifts. Different paths. Different creations. That's what makes it so beautiful.

Our God-given gifts should not be used to make people live in fear, control, or manipulation. If that's how you may see some people using their gifts, I would walk the other way. Actually, run! Because I don't believe that is coming from God. God wants you to empower yourself. I believe HE or SHE wants you to feel the undeniable truth from within your own heart. The love for oneself and others. If someone is telling you they are the only ones who have the answers or are the "chosen ones," I want you to know that is absolutely not true. Because so do you. You just have to trust your own heart. And remember, with God, ANYTHING is possible.

CHAPTER 10

Angels

"Fear not: for heaven and heart combined is the womb of magic itself."
– The Angels

Angels! Another one of my favorite things to talk about these days. They are talked about in the Bible a little under 300 times. They are also mentioned in most religions throughout the world, including Judaism, Christianity, Hinduism, and Islam. And let me tell you, it's all fascinating to me. They are talked about with different names, but all have a very similar tone. They are the messengers of God. If you google the word angel, it is defined as a "spiritual being believed to act as an attendant, agent, or messenger of God."

Growing up in a Christian church, I definitely have heard of angels and the stories in the Bible. But I didn't know a lot more than those stories. I am not even sure I knew about many archangels and how they are truly the messengers of God. They were another thing to me that felt as though they were way up in the sky somewhere far away, and they only came down during the time that the Bible stories were being written. And they only came to the people who deserved to see them. I thought that one day, in heaven, I might see one. But it felt so far away from me, even though I have loved angels since I was a little girl. And to be honest, I don't think I gave it much more thought. It seemed like stories I felt so disconnected from, but yet they were so beautiful to think about all at the same time.

What is interesting to me about all of this is that they are mentioned throughout the Bible in so many beautiful stories. If so many people believe these stories, why does it seem so crazy to think that they are actually here and always have been helping us all now? It shouldn't seem that crazy to think that God does have His messengers here to help with our everyday lives, and there are a lot of them. They are incredibly powerful, incredibly healing, deeply loving, and they are here to help humanity with all the directions life takes us down. They want us to know they are much closer to all of us than we may realize or even think is possible. They hold the magic that we, as humans, can create the miracles we deeply desire on this planet. They want to help transform our everyday lives into the heaven-on-earth shift that we know in our deepest hearts can be possible. It's the shift that is coming and the miracles that want to play out for humanity in general. It's time to really get to know them and understand how the higher vibrational frequencies of the angel realm are protecting us, guiding us, and trying to encourage us to get those lights to the absolute brightest possible path.

When I truly awakened, one thing that really started to show itself to me was the angels. Now, guys, I promise you that from the bottom of my heart, I thought I was going crazy, too. So, if you are reading this and thinking to yourself, *What?* I get it! I promise. I had to work through all of this. I was *terrified* to talk about it. Sometimes, I still am because it's not something that I can just announce over Thanksgiving dinner or talk to Karen on the sidelines at baseball about. It seemed so dramatically different from how I was living previously. Or how people knew me. It just seemed like no one would believe it. I was so scared to share this with anyone besides people who also could see/feel the angels. And I searched and searched for the people who could. I had so many questions. But I also felt safe in sharing what I was hearing and believing with those people. I felt so safe to share the truth that I knew in my heart had been there all along. I am very thankful for those connections and people at that time. They helped me in many ways. They shared their own gifts and their own truths, and I'll always be so thankful the angels guided me to all those people and still do almost every day in some way, shape, or form.

I felt like, at that time of first awakening, I was seeing the outside world just spin around me, even though I had never felt so connected, present, calm, and blissful about life. I felt that I was looking at everything that was happening around me in a different way. I thought deeply about my kids, their purpose, relationships, people, politics, war, and religion. I felt a deep sense that it all seemed so crazy. We were all so similar, yet so different. Why was there any pain, trauma, anger, war, or greed in general? Why couldn't people see that we all did come from the same God/source? I had an overwhelming feeling that it was a part of my purpose to help reconnect people's minds and hearts—just like so many of you.

I wanted to help them remember their own inner truth and spiritual connection that they so desperately need to feel whole. I knew I was going to start talking and teaching about the angels, even though it was terrifying and was dramatically different from my previous life. Would anyone listen or care? Would they be interested in any of this whatsoever? Or would everyone think I'd gone crazy? Maybe I had. But I would take this crazy if that's what it was because it was so beautiful. I felt so much healing and filled with so much love, not only for myself but for all those around me. It's rising higher than ever before, and I deeply share my empathy for all those who need me the most.

I could see through people's anger like never before. I felt calmer and more present with every single connection, from little hands to big, open hearts. It was the start of my own version of heaven on earth. I saw so much magic and beauty every day. People started to just show up on my path out of nowhere, and I knew they were being placed there for a reason. I started feeling more comfortable sharing my own gifts with friends, family, or anyone who I knew was being sent for an angel message and from the angels themselves. It's still amazing to see who shows up. I am so grateful to all those who let me share and keep an open mind and heart while doing so.

There are many different types of angels. As I mentioned earlier, we all have teams of angels supporting us in life, whether we are aware of them or not. We have spirit guides, guardian angels, and loved ones. Then there are also the Archangels. They are here to help everyone. They are beings with a very high vibrational frequency and light patterns. They are here to help bring up old wounds at times and to bring forward the healing power that we are all capable of bringing to light. If I had to use one word to describe the archangels, I would use empowerment. They are helping the world transition in such a beautiful way, and they want everyone to know that they are capable of helping every human transform into their own brightest light—the version of themselves that is begging to break free and come alive.

They are non-denominational beings that have served humanity for so many eons. They want you to know and understand that calling in their light is a straight connection to God Himself/Herself. You can feel safe, protected, loved, and ready to step into your own true divine power/gifts with their helping hand. They are friends of yours. They see all you do: your grief, your love, your worries, and your troubles. They want to help lead you to a path that you were meant for, not one that ties you deeply into more hurt, anger, or resentment.

Being a spiritual human does not mean things will always just be easy. Human life is filled with challenges and lessons. These all grow and expand our soul's consciousness. We can't see this or understand it from this viewpoint, but our lessons actually teach our souls. We are here to go through challenges and tribulations at times because we need to grow, expand, and heal. This can feel so unfair, challenging, and confusing for us at times. But when we heal our hurt, we can expand and help lead others to do the same. Our empathy opens wider, and we can circle back to teach others what they have forgotten about themselves. It's a trial for others to really bring back their deepest desires.

Break free and understand we are here with physical bodies, but our spiritual self wants to really break free. We forget that, at times, we are actually spiritual beings having a physical experience, not the other way around!

What the angels can really bring to us in this lifetime is the love of oneself and the ability to feel whole and worthy and really unravel the deep pain that is buried away inside of us for many reasons. They can help inspire you to be creative, joyful, and present. They can unlock the truth inside of your own heart and really push forward those possibilities your heart wants you to really experience. They can help you develop an enthusiastic spirit that draws you to all the magic you want to create in your life and all the possibilities of endless love for not only others but yourself. They are a great connection to God and remind you why you're really here. They want to open the doorway to heaven on earth and allow you to break free from any negativity blocking you on this path. They want you to shine higher than ever before and really understand how and why they can help you.

The stories we have all grown up with and have heard about the angelic realm are beautiful ways to inspire us about what is truly possible. It doesn't need to feel so far away and removed from us. We don't need to feel as though their angelic wings are so high above us that they will never bring us the truth. They are here, standing next to you at this very moment. All we need to do is call them into our hearts and allow them to help us. To help bring you hope for all of humanity. I promise if you are reading these words, the angels have guided you to do so. Even if it was just your curiosity bringing you to this book, you were meant to read this.

Our voices have so much power, but so do our thoughts. That is where we can really feel a transformation of ourselves if we can magnetically call in the angels and help clear our thoughts and old belief systems that may no longer serve our highest good. When we use our angel friends for reprogramming, we are clearing and making a path to our greatest potential. We are *all* capable of experiencing an abundance of love, health, financial freedom, and other endless possibilities. They truly can bring forward such a spark of joy and love into your everyday life. They need you to understand that their voices echo a lot of what you already know deep from within. They can help lead you right to that own voice. Your own gifts. Your own power. They can create shifts from the inside that expand our hearts, make us feel incredibly connected, and bring forward so much love that will radiate for all to see/hear.

Humanity is truly at a changing point. The earth is creating and shifting and bringing in so many changes. It's time for humanity to understand that collectively, we need to shift into a higher vibrational frequency that serves humanity the highest. The love frequency is straight from God Himself. It's possible. We are the ones that are bringing about this change. Why did we want to come into this lifetime? We wanted to see the changes happen and help assist with what is possible.

So many Christians believe in the second coming of Christ. This has been talked about a lot throughout history, especially lately, all over the world. But what if we switched our mindset and asked the big question, "What if He is already here?" Maybe it is different from what has been translated by certain religions throughout history. Christ consciousness.

The consciousness of Christ Himself is already here. I do believe that. I'm sure so many of you do as well. His connection is delivering the messages of spreading love, light, connection, and unity. We need to understand that He is not someone or somebody who is judging what religion you receive His love in or what your belief system is about Him. He wants all of us to really dive deeper into the connection from within to God Himself. He wants us to understand we can all receive His healings, teachings, and connections with unity at large. He is completely about spreading love and light and diving deep into His own connection with God's lights. He presented Himself and traveled to teach people what is possible for all of us. We all have healing hands with the capabilities of lights from above. His connection to the angelic realm is a huge one. He felt what was possible and tried to guide others to feel and do the same. When we open our minds and hearts to what is possible, miracles create a domino effect of love and light. He is helping lead the way to Christ consciousness, and the angels are a big part of that as well.

We don't need to be scared of what is possible. We don't need to act or deliver a certain amount of hostility and judgment for others when they may feel differently. And honestly, even if you're reading this and not believing one word, that is okay! I promise, I totally get it. This will not resonate with everyone. You are allowed to stand in your own truth. Believe what your own heart is telling you. I will still cheer you on, send you love, and root for you.

We need to unite with our love for one another. We need to understand there is no right or wrong way to get into heaven. We need to serve others with a Christlike mindset and bring forward that unity and love for one another. A Christlike mindset is someone who recognizes the truth from within. They are able to see a higher perspective and deliver their own soul's voice in many ways. It's someone who loves deeply and presents their light in the most authentic and vulnerable way. It's real, raw, and full of human emotion, and truly here to help lead the way for your own soul's highest good. Christ is pure heart and love.

There are so many angelic beings and friends who want to help us. That is why prayer, meditation, and the connection with the divine are so important. The power we have to ask for help, guidance, and truth is unbreakable. We just need to ask so they can deliver what they want for you in this lifetime. They are here to assist us with even the small day-to-day tasks that we can feel guilty for asking for divine help or intervention with. They want us to know that life is meant to feel alive and well. There is nothing too small or too big. They want to help us with all human life experiences. Their love is never going to stop trying to connect with us because you have asked one too many questions, or you feel as though you need answers for simple math questions (*ha!*). They will be here to assist us and guide us through and for all things. They want a connection and friendship with you. Their love is truly a feeling and a glimpse into heaven. Let's dive into how we can call on them and who is here to help us!

CHAPTER 11
My First Angel Connection: Archangel Gabriel

"Our voice is what can connect us to the most powerful truths from within us. Speaking freely with love and compassion for oneself and others. But most importantly, speaking from the truth. It's true enlightenment."
– Archangel Gabriel

I researched everything I could about angels, people who also felt connected to angels, and why I felt connected to angels and other people felt connected to different spiritual gifts. I knew I needed validation. I reached out to a few other people who also seemed to have some spiritual gifts connected to angels specifically. I would ask for readings, take classes, ask them questions, and would be blown away by what every single one of them would tell me. They all told me the same thing, even though none of them knew me, none of them knew each other, and they lived in all different parts of the world.

They would all say something along the lines of, "Hey, you really do know those archangels!" I would laugh and say, "Yes, I think I do." Even though I still felt so crazy, it was hard for me to even talk about it out loud because it was something that was *so* different from what I was usually talking about. I wasn't going down the streets shouting, "I'm friends with the archangels, everyone!"

The angel who would show up so strongly every single time with not only myself but everyone who I was learning from, and receiving angel readings myself was Archangel Gabriel. Gabriel is the angel of communication, so it makes sense that he was really trying to connect with me first. I knew he was leading this angel team for me, and I could tell he was really excited that I was finally paying attention to him.

Archangel Gabriel's energy was so loving that it would sometimes bring me to instant tears. Incredibly powerful, Gabriel really helps people use their voices in many ways. He helps with creative projects, communication, childhood traumas, and anything that you want to bring to life in this world through relationships, projects at work, ideas, and creativity. Gabriel is amazing with this. That's why he is still so important to me and always will be. That's why I still connect with him, have him lead a lot of my messages, and teach others about him. He is powerful and wants to help anyone who asks him.

The first time I really sat down and felt an overwhelming feeling (literally like someone was pushing me to the computer, sitting me down, and wanting me to write), I knew it was him. He was helping me really focus on opening my voice and letting out what needed to come out. I knew that what I was writing wasn't really my own writing or thoughts but messages from Gabriel. I still have a lot of those first words and communication. I still go back and re-read them and feel blown away. I'm so glad this was a way of him teaching me what I could do, how I could connect, how our relationship would grow, and what was even possible. It was as though he was my first angel mentor. My teacher. I just couldn't really see my mentor, ya know, physically, in the room (ha-ha).

I would often joke with him and once again feel like an insane person because I would get answers back. I'm like, *"How in the world am I ever, ever going to share this, Gabriel? The world will laugh at me. This is insane!*

He would always reassure me, *"Your voice is what will resonate with a lot of people. You are not untruthful; you are relatable, and you are someone people will believe. You have to have courage and strength in this. You have to believe in yourself. Your voice is needed. More people will be accepting of this, and they themselves are starting to feel the breakthroughs and connections and need more guidance with their own spiritual gifts."*

I trusted in this. (Obviously, I'm writing a book!) But the more I connected, the more I learned from other people who also connected to angels, the more I trusted myself. I also found some great mentors at that time which helped me understand my gift in the first place. It's like I said earlier, the more we use this gift, the stronger it becomes. The more we trust, the more we can feel the truth and hear what we are meant to hear.

I will be honest; I don't even know if it won't ever NOT sound crazy to me. Truly, if you had told me just a few years ago that I would be writing about the archangels and their messages, I would have laughed so hard and wouldn't have believed it for one second. I keep bringing this up for a couple of reasons. I know there are a lot of people who are questioning if they are crazy or if they are also feeling a stronger connection to the angels or their own divine gifts. I also want everyone to know I never once thought, *Hey, this will be so easy and cool to share! Wooohooo.* I was *terrified* to talk about this. Deeply terrified. I questioned it all.

I also have family members who were telling me this was bad or wrong because they were told this by someone else from a religious standpoint. I had to work through a lot. It didn't happen overnight for me. It took a couple of years before I even got up the nerve to share my gifts with anyone else. I kept it locked away. But I was so excited to connect to that part of me each and every day. It was like I was living in my own little secret world. It felt so safe, filled with love, guidance, and miracles. I thought, *Well, I can connect, but I don't really have to share this with anyone else.*

Then, once again, Gabriel would tell me, *"Wrong. Your voice is meant to be heard with these messages and truths. People need this now* more than ever before, and they are ready now. You are meant to speak and help others connect. You are meant to be a messenger."

It seemed way too scary and way too different from what I was doing, so I told him, *"I have a lifestyle blog. I am a mom. I hang out at eight-year-old baseball games, practices, school functions, and neighborhood parties. I am not an angel messenger, Gabriel!"*

He said, *"You will do this your own way. It will resonate with many people who need this and also are experiencing this for themselves. Their divine selves are awakening, at large."*

As my connection grew stronger and stronger, especially with Gabriel leading the way, it was as if my soul and physical body couldn't keep all these words, messages, stories, and experiences in any longer. It was as if I was bursting at the seams. My throat would actually become hot and burn. I would have tingles on my forehead and my throat and an overwhelming feeling. I would be around certain people, and I knew with every ounce in me that I was meant to tell them things with so much love and heart involved. I knew people were showing up out of nowhere for certain reasons. I knew people randomly would start talking about this stuff out of nowhere, but none of this was a coincidence. It was meant to be.

I was opening and shifting into the person I was always meant to be. My soul was leading the way and taking over in a way. I knew the angels were also helping me and placing me where I needed to be and who I needed to be around, and I started to pay attention to all this. I also started to pay attention to just so many signs every day that it would almost be laughable! It was outrageous sometimes, to the point it was unbelievable. So much was happening; I couldn't ignore it. I knew I would have to step into my true power and be okay with starting to speak about it. I knew I would have to start authentically being me. Which is not always easy to do, thanks to our egos and human selves.

I remember the first time I told my husband about all this. He had known me for over a decade, and giving angel messages was not something that I previously had talked about. He also is a very logical, very structured, very type A personality. He works in finance, and his brain works *very* differently from mine. It always has.

Throughout the years, he would hear me say time after time, "*Trust me!*" which would drive him nuts. I often had a feeling about a place, person, or situation. I didn't have a spreadsheet or a logical reason why; I just trusted deeply what I was feeling in certain situations. So, in a way, he was always used to this part of me in some sense. I had no idea then that I was using my intuition in those moments, my sensitivities, my divine wisdom, and my inner knowing deep from within me. I just didn't have the words or context to understand what was happening. This happens to so many of us!

I remember finally sharing with him after a few months of all of this growing stronger and stronger. I said, "I know this sounds absolutely *crazy,* but I really think this is happening."

He looked at me, and I will never forget his response. "If anyone is talking to angels, Ashley, it's you."

I still can remember where we were and how I felt those words. He believed me. And let me tell you, that's not easy for a very logical spreadsheet brain to do. But his believing me and supporting me was also angelic guidance. They knew I would need that support in those moments and at that time.

My husband is not someone who is very emotionally charged. Like I said, he has a math brain, is logical, and is always on a mission. This can be hard for a sensitive, emotional, and heart-centered person to always be around or connect with. I'm bringing this up because I feel like I want to share this part of my story. We are so different, but I need that logical and structured brain. And he needs my sensitive heart. So, he did not even skip a beat, and I knew he believed me. He has never doubted me once, even from the very beginning—ever. He thought this was all so cool! Which at times, I would be like, "Honey, you can't just blurt this out or share with other people. I'm not ready to do that yet. Not everyone will understand this. This is not a party trick (*haha*)." I also knew he was fascinated by everything I was sharing with him. It was fun, but I only shared it with him slowly over time. It was like dipping your toes in the water. There was so much that was not only coming out of me but also things I was learning from books and teachers. So, I shared little pieces but didn't overwhelm him with constant angel or spiritual teachings.

I want to share this because I think it's so normal when one person is awakening that they think the other person in the relationship needs to get on their level as well. Or you want to share all the things that you know are absolutely true, such as things that you can see/hear/smell/or just know. I want to remind you that we all have our own journeys. His awakening may take way longer in this lifetime, or maybe he won't even experience it. (In this lifetime). His soul came here to grow and expand, but not in the same way mine did. So you can't force people to understand where your soul level is—where your consciousness is. They are on their own journey. I would encourage you, though, if you are experiencing this in your relationship, to find people who are on your soul level. Reach out to friends, teachers, and mentors, or join a new community that is like-minded so you can talk about all the things you want to talk about! It's so important because you are going to want to surround yourself with truth, validation, and heart. You want that higher vibrational energy to connect with, so make sure to find some people you can share with! Find your frequency family. They are out there, I promise!

I feel like Gabriel is reminding me to share this at this very moment, you can also ask for his assistance with this. Ask him to lead you to new friendships, communities, and places you can explore that will bring your soul that deep connection and longing you're looking for. If you are married or in a relationship, I'm not talking about divorcing your partner and moving forward so you can find this; I'm suggesting that while you're awakening and deeply wanting that soul connection, ask Gabriel to place friendships on the path for you that you can talk about the things you really want to talk about and be the real you. Have the conversations you really want to have. This is so important!

Or maybe you're the one who will start a small group in your own community! Yoga classes, walking out in nature, and book clubs are all great ways to start small groups in your community or find new friends who will share similar interests! I started a coffee and connection group with four women in my area. We meet twice a month and share our spiritual gifts, common interests, struggles, achievements, mom life, and so much more. It's been a true blessing to have this space to be able to show up completely 100% authentically being me. I know they feel the same.

Gabriel can help lead you to these types of relationships with likeminded individuals. Pray about it; you never know who else is craving this type of connection. And I will be honest: when I first awakened, and my spiritual gifts started to show up in a big way, I used to think, oh my gosh, there is no one else like this in my area. There will be no one that is as strange as me. (*Ha!*) Wrong. There are so many awakened souls that live right around me that are equally craving this type of connection. So don't let fear of what others may think or say stand in the way! Your people are out there. You never know who else is thinking or questioning things just like this. They need you just like you need them. It's time to start showing up authentically *you*, If I can do it, I promise so can you!

Gabriel is a fun and friendly angel but also can be serious in such a loving way. I love his energy. He wants me to share that he really is like a vocal coach or best friend to you. He wants you to use your voice. Share the things that have haunted you or that you never felt like you were allowed to talk about, explore, or understand. He wants you to know that befriending yourself, the angels, and God will make you feel as though you can accomplish anything. It won't always be easy, but he will help lead you. He is powerful and empowering about childhood and our inner-childlike playfulness. He wants us to understand that we are able to feel like that our entire life if we allow ourselves to do so. We are meant to be playful and see the world the way children do, the impact they make on our hearts. He says we should remember that our inner child is still here. No matter if your childhood was happy or not, he wants to help you heal the wounds and bring out that playful, childish energy so you laugh and use your imagination. He said that is so powerful! He is saying that the worlds we create with our hearts and imagination beam with light, which is why children beam with light.

Let your imagination explore all possibilities and really lead with the most creative version of yourself. Paint a picture, talk to a friend, or explore a new part of the world. Adult play can look different from childhood play, but that same magical happiness can still be there. Allow yourself to know and understand you deserve and are worthy of happiness. Children know and understand this up until a certain age, depending on their experience. Gabriel says to remind yourself that you are deserving no matter what you have been through. You are capable of leading yourself back to that path that you wish you had a chance on. It's never too late to accept your path and surrender your light to the right one. God. We learn from our mistakes. Don't beat yourself up; just get back up and try again.

Exploring different parts of us is also what makes things seem more magical. Knowing yourself is important because it can lead you to where you need to be. Gabriel wants us to enjoy the spiritual sides of ourselves. Don't be afraid of it, as there's nothing to be afraid of. We can talk ourselves into circles by being afraid that we aren't supposed to do something, or this is the only way we can connect to our spiritual self. He said to not think so much about what or how to connect to that part of us and forget the "rules." We are meant to know this side of us. We came here to feel connected, but we forgot. We are conditioned to think and act a certain way. Remembering who we really are is the entire point of us being here. We must learn to love our soul selves, lead with heart and compassion, and help others to do the same. We forget that we all come from a lot of the same energy source—God.

We ask so much about ourselves and others. We put so much pressure on ourselves, and what Gabriel is saying is to relax, have fun, and enjoy this life. It is such a blessing to be here, even though it can be difficult as well. He knows and understands this. Regrets are what most people experience on the other side. They forget why they came, who they really are, and what they really wanted to accomplish or experience in this lifetime. No one gets punished for not doing the job they came to do. You will just experience your growth in different ways in heaven. Also, know that your jobs can simply be helping another person see a different viewpoint, assisting a neighbor, or allowing your children to be who they really are. It does not need to be a crazy mission. Everyone has different plans and things they want to learn and experience. Don't beat yourself up that your plan is not like someone else's. Your connection to yourself and others is a big part of what your soul wants in this lifetime. Simplicity is also an energetic footprint and will help you connect with nature and God. Explore. Don't feel the heaviness of what the world is telling you, but explore your own truth.

Gabriel is also saying to breathe, take time to create things, and learn to stay present. That is a gift in itself. Learning to breathe and enjoy the moment that is in front of you is something that a lot of people forget to do. There is so much beauty and magic in everyday life in the connections with others, the trees, and the sunshine. We forget those simple little feelings and things, but they are actually really strong connections and reminders of who we really are. Don't forget to be grateful for this life. You are a strong and very powerful being. You are capable of pivoting, starting fresh, and creating the life you know you deserve. Your patterns of everyday life can change, so break free of the old ways and realign with your new energy. Use fresh energy. You can break through to the person you know you can be. Think of this like charging your soul and getting an energy upgrade.

Gabriel also wants to remind us that laughter is important on a vibrational level. We should find that joy and connection and not take ourselves so seriously. We all make mistakes, but figuring out what makes you laugh or what makes you happy is really important. So, take your kids and just let them run free, explore, and create, and remember to do it yourself as well. We start to feel that heaviness, burden, and burnout when our soul feels trapped. We just don't understand this. Gabriel says we should figure out where the heaviness or overwhelmed feelings come from. Do we need to downsize? Do we need a different lifestyle or plan? Do we need to go on more adventures? Do we need to create something? Do we need to ask for more help or allow our vulnerability to come through? Do we need new relationships or friendships? It's okay to just be you. Breathe again, take more walks, and enjoy your children and your animals. We make life so difficult because we put so many expectations on ourselves from other people. Don't worry or think too much about it. You don't have to march into the job you hate every single day. Can you start praying and looking for a new one? Sit down with paper and start writing what you really want in your life. Call Gabriel in with you, and he will help you come up with some new ideas.

Your life is something that won't always be easy; it's not meant to be. There are lessons for people to learn while they are here. But life should be loving, fun, and beautiful. It can be easy at times, but most importantly, there should just be a natural flow and trust in you every day. Appreciate what we have been given by God and move forward, knowing you have the power to create the life you really desire. It may be as simple as noticing and being present more in the life you are already living.

He is saying humans really focus on what they are told they need to do and how they aren't good enough and ask themselves, *Where will my love be?* Or *How do I meet my soulmate?* Gabriel is saying we should return to the JOY of life, and all this will start becoming less heavy. Use your heart and voice and tell people what you really want or maybe what you don't. Speak with kindness but the reassurance of oneself. You are in control of yourself, and your thoughts can produce the outcomes you want. Think highly of your worth. Gabriel can help us find that piece that we know is there but feels like it's missing, such as our voices, our childlike joy, and our creativity.

Gabriel is such a beautiful angel. He has such beautiful energy. And I personally think he is a lot of fun. Some people connect with his energy and feel like it's more feminine, but I can feel both masculine and feminine energy. He is light but determined. Playful but honest. Creative. He wants to open your throat chakras and really allow your voice to communicate in an honest, authentic, heart-led way. He loves helping children and can help you heal your own inner child wounds.

Call on Gabriel anytime! That is what I want everyone to understand the most in this book. I'm not special in any way, shape, or form because I can give angel messages. You can, too! They are here for everyone. I would love for you to deepen your connection with the angels while reading this book. I promise you don't need me, although I'm more than happy to help you! If this is something that is brand new to you, like it was for me, let's connect with some exercise/homework while reading.

A great exercise to help with this would be to sit down and write to Gabriel.

> *Archangel Gabriel, I call you into work with your beautiful bright light for my highest good and everyone involved. I ask to be covered in God's light. I want to connect to your high vibrational energy, and I would love to return my heart to that joy I feel may be missing in certain areas of my life. I pray that you will show and lead me with the steps I need to take to get there. I ask that you not only help lead me but also show me signs, communicate with me, and really take my hand as I open up my heart to your energy and healing capabilities. Help me understand my higher self, my highest path, and how to get there. If there is healing I need to work through, help me in a loving, tender way. I'm thankful for your love, your connection, and your guidance. I'm excited to get to know you better!*

WRITING TO GABRIEL

1. Gabriel, I would love to use my voice more in these areas of my life (specify). Can you help me understand how to do it? (Write out this exact question and then write down the first thing that pops into your mind. Nothing is crazy. Just write!)

_____
_____
_____
_____

2. Gabriel, I know that my inner child is wounded in many ways. What is something that I can do to start healing these wounds on a profound level?

_____
_____
_____
_____

3. Gabriel, I'm seeking more creativity in my life. What steps can I start to take to open this part of myself up more?

_____
_____
_____
_____

4. Gabriel, do you have anything you want to share with me personally?

_____
_____
_____
_____

I do want to note one thing when working with the Archangels. They will *never* say anything negative. They will *never* tell you to do something bad. They will actually *never* tell you what to do. You have free will, but they will help guide you. They will fill you with love and validation on a soul level. If you feel you are being told to do a specific action, are hearing negative thoughts, or are saying something bad, it's not an angel influencing you. Most likely, it's our own ego getting in the way. Archangels will give you the truth, but not in a negative way. It's more of a validation of what you already know deeply within. Remember, they have a very high vibrational frequency. They are full of so much love. They are not here to tell you exactly what to do every second of the day. They want to empower you to learn and trust your heart and divine self, your own higher self's truth, and your own soul. They are healing friends, guides, teachers, and mentors. They love you!

CHAPTER 12

Archangel Michael

"Negativity can flood our minds. But the truth will allow it to escape. Don't confuse your own truth for negativity. Your mind can play tricks on you, but your heart knows the answers. Stay still, connect to this part of you, and watch your world transform."
– Archangel Michael

Archangel Michael is another angel I felt deeply connected with right away! He is another angel I had heard of but knew so little about. Someone long ago told me to pray with him when I traveled. So I always did. It's funny to think about now because I would always say this quietly to myself: *Archangel Michael, please be with me and protect me while I am traveling,* calling him in, but I don't really know if I understood why, who he was, or what I was doing, but there was something deep within me that trusted that little piece of advice long ago.

I absolutely love Michael's energy. Every time I feel him around me or connect with him (which is every day because I constantly call him in for protection, not only for me but also for my family), I feel a big wave of high energy and protection. He has more masculine energy, and I always envision him with this giant, beautiful light and armor on. I know every picture out there is exactly this with Michael, so maybe that's why my human self is painting this picture, but I feel it, too. The thing that I think most people would be surprised to learn about Michael is that even though his energy seems so massive and masculine and comes with so much protection, there's an extraordinary amount of kindness, patience, love, and listening energy with him. I adore his energy and am so thankful for him. He is a major presence in my everyday life, with my messages to other people and myself. I know he is helping lead all this as well. He is excited for other people to get to know him, call on him, and really understand how he can help you in your everyday life.

Michael wants everyone to know and understand that his power and presence can help transform your life. He can help lead you to your higher self, your confident self, and your passionate self. He can help real-life miracles come through into your everyday life. He will always be there to help anyone in need and really wants to work with as many people as he can in this lifetime.

Pictures of Michael often depict him as a masculine angel with armor on. He wants us to know he does love that people think of him in this way because he is a protector of many things, places, and people. He does have the power of God's magical protection. He will help you and your family in any time of need, danger, or urgency. He can't always promise what the outcome will be, but he is there, protecting and leading you to what is meant to be. We may have a very hard time rationalizing this in certain and unfair situations. But he will never leave you when you call on him in moments when you feel scared or afraid. We will never, ever understand this with our human minds, but what is meant to be is to be. It's out of our hands as humans a lot of the time.

Michael is also someone who really wants people to clear out their negativity. He wants people to understand that masculine energy is not always the way it may present itself on earth. Masculine energy should be powerful but also come from the heart. Masculine energy to Michael is someone who listens, understands, and is patient but also incredibly powerful in a compassionate, leader-type way in all different situations. He is saying that true masculine energy is someone who knows how to lead others but not in a manipulative or controlling way. He feels so strongly about this. He wants people to understand that, sometimes, when we use the word masculine, we are using it out of context because of what we have been told to think masculine is. He believes there are so many men out there who strongly need to understand this, and he is really trying to help. They have forgotten about leading with their heart. It doesn't mean that they need to be sensitive 24/7; it just means they need to know their own truth and who they really are. They need to be in true alignment with themselves in heart and mind. That is, being truly masculine. He wants people to take responsibility for this and really understand what he is presenting.

Real men come from boys who are raised to listen to others' thoughts and feelings. They are allowed to express their own hearts and ways of thinking. There are so many men who have gotten lost in their true heart's expressions. Their hearts are locked and covered up, and they are told not to experience that part of them. He says he feels like this is changing and starting to really uncover a lot of truths. It's a good thing and a good time to reflect on these changes and patterns from within. He wants to help you! He is passionate about helping men and parents raising boys to really understand what masculine means.

Being masculine is about being powerful. We need the masculine leaders of the world to return to that piece of them that has a heart and mind connection. It's a beautiful thing he is reminding us of. Men need confidence, leadership skills, and to really know who they are and what they want, without the ego or hurt getting in the way. It's possible; we just have to be willing to do the work or really let our emotions be expressed in the way they need to be at times. We must be authentic. Michael knows this can be scary at times, maybe even confusing. But he is saying this in the most simplistic of ways. It's okay to be a leader and operate from your heart. It does not have to be one or the other.

Michael wants you to lead your own life from within. He wants to help remind you that you are capable of truly diving into any situation you are faced with from the person you know you truly are. Leadership and strength are all part of this. Allow yourself to really understand who you really are and what you really want in life, and be able to speak and lead yourself to these things. He wants you to feel as though you are promoting yourself to your next phase of life, releasing old patterns but really bringing forward the strength you carry, your determination, and your fire spirit. That is the part of you that can lead you into any situation that your heart desires. He wants to encourage you to try new things, listen to others' opinions, and be able to live in the moment. Don't let your rage win, but know it's okay to learn and grow from past mistakes. It's okay that sometimes we mistake our ego for our soul's voice. We are learning and growing, expanding at all times. You just need to understand that your soul really is the part of you that can sync all this together.

Michael is an angel who speaks passionately and honestly. He has a lot of fire and strength. He is someone who can turn your entire world upside down because you will really start to understand your own strength, your own inner validation, and how you can rely less on outside factors. He is surprisingly easy to work with. He wants you to know and understand you have everything it already takes to connect to him, and he is waiting for your connection!

I think in today's world, with everything we have going on and the different opinions, wars, dictatorships, and religions, we can easily get lost. We forget so willingly because we have been conditioned to. It is a part of our experience here on earth to really set things aside for a minute and ask yourself, *What feels true to you?* I feel like this is where Michael can also be such a great friend, mentor, and guide to help you realize you have so much strength and truth inside. Once you can really push play on curiosity and allow yourself to really trust yourself, our world will change for the better. He wants to build that inner confidence so you can really trust and discern what is true for you. You are capable of producing, starting, and becoming so much no matter what road you came from or what you've been told you can or cannot become—although sometimes we hold ourselves back. Michael can help evaluate what it is you really want. He likes to help clear out the negative thoughts in our minds. The ones that we are tired of playing over and over. Allow those patterns to be placed over to Michael. Ask him to clear the negativity of your mind and help you change your own mindset. He wants nothing more than for you to feel like your most confident self. He wants you to feel like anything is possible because it truly is.

When I first started working with Michael, I instantly felt protected. It was almost like someone like Thor with wings was standing next to me. *Ha-ha*. I don't know why I envision this, but I always joke with him that if he looks like Chris Hemsworth, can he please just show me? (Yes, you can joke with angels.) I felt like a very strong but soft presence. And I think that's why he brought up masculinity earlier in this chapter. He wants people to know and understand you can be masculine yet so connected to your heart. That mind-heart connection is what the world needs. And it's VERY powerful. Leading with love, truth, and honor of oneself is what will make a difference in all areas of your life.

I call Michael every single time I connect to the angels or do any sort of reading. Every single time, he is the one I first call on. I know I'm incredibly protected, but there is something about calling him right away that makes me feel like I'm extra protected. It never hurts to call on Michael at any time and watch your life transform magically. He will help wash away those negative thoughts and lead you to true confidence that starts from within. I encourage everyone reading this to start working with him!

WRITING TO MICHAEL

1. Ask Michael, "Michael, what is it that is blocking me from true confidence from within?" (Whatever pops up, even if it's so silly, write it down, even if it's a picture, a feeling, or a story. Trust it and write it down.)

_____
_____
_____
_____

2. Michael, let me feel your protection and love!

3. Michael, what can I do better to align myself with more positive thoughts?

4. Archangel Michael, please help me with any anxiety or negativity. I ask you to clear anything that continues to block me. I know this won't be easy, but learning to break these patterns is what my true self really wants!

CHAPTER 13
Archangel Raphael

"It's time to take control of your health, mind, and spirit. For when we do not fully express our truest and deepest emotions and expressions of who we are, they get trapped and stored deep within. Causing underlying ailments at various degrees. It's time to unlock this part of you and stand tall and proud of what you are able to express. Your ability to be set free will make a profound impact on your overall health."
– Archangel Raphael

Another angel I love dearly is Archangel Raphael. He is best known as the healer angel. Although all the angels are incredibly healing, Raphael is known as the angel who can help physically heal and help with healing the heart. I always call in Raphael for angel readings and try to help teach people about him when they are praying for other people and themselves, especially when it comes to health matters, physical conditions, and relationship problems. I have always loved to teach more about this beautiful angel.

Raphael is usually seen or felt with a bright green light. So, if you start to call him into your prayer or meditation, envision a bright green light around you or whoever else you are praying for. This can help us feel even more connected. To me, Raphael is incredibly vibrant, healing, and full of love (even though they all are), and really wants to show you what is possible to physically heal ourselves.

Raphael is great to call on and ask for help with relationship issues as well. When matters of the heart impact us, call in Raphael. Help him clear out negativity or things that are holding you back from seeing clearly what you need to do to move past this situation and embrace your higher self. It's normal for our human heart to get stuck in cycles, patterns, and situations that really aren't providing us with the best representation of who we really are. We are allowing others to validate our own heart and truth when he will remind us it all starts from within our own heart and how powerful we really are. When you feel that love inside of you growing like never before, that is when all the cycles, patterns, and manipulation of others can stop the hurt that you desperately are trying to get away from.

This does not have to be just romantic relationships. This is also friendships, family matters, and any situation that is really affecting you and your heart. Ask for his guidance and allow him to really show and open up new doors, signs, and power from within you. I feel like he wants me to remind all of us that we are the architects of our own doing. Our hearts, relationships, and patterns are all under our control, no matter the path we have walked. Yes, we may have learned things, been led to trust and have had that shattered, and so on, but we can heal and learn that the truest version of deep love is inside our hearts.

When we realize how powerful and full of love we really are, miracles truly start taking shape. When we align to our higher self and lead with the light that we were created to have, the best relationships come our way. You're now living at a higher level. You no longer want to serve others with lower vibrations than your own, and you know how much love and life you can give because you already know what is inside of you. You feel it, see it, and embrace it all around you.

I feel like this is the love and alignment our children deserve as well.

They need to see that their parents love themselves and feel love, and they can pour that into the children so they can grow up feeling and knowing what they deserve as well. And it all cycles around. It helps everyone involved. And the best part is you are incredibly capable and incredibly deserving of love from within. And deserve to be valued, treasured, and adored outside as well. It all matters deeply, and that is how we can have the healthiest relationships in our lives. It's deeply important!

Raphael can really help heal physically as well. He can assist with anything from small ailments to the larger ones causing major issues. Call him in your prayer and your healing. Feel his light over your body and ask him to remove anything that no longer deserves to be in your energy field. He also can help show you things that you may not even be aware of that are stuck or something that maybe you need to go to the doctor to check on. Ask him to send you to the right doctors!

Sometimes, we have an idea that something may not be right, but we keep pushing through. Or maybe a doctor is telling us one thing, but something feels like there are problems at the root causing whatever is being described to you. Trust yourself. Advocate for yourself and pray.

The biggest part of working with any of the angels is having faith to begin with. I understand why this might be considered crazy, but why not try? No one has to know, and it really can help you every day. Remember that YOU are truly the miracle worker to begin with. Aligning with this feeling and allowing yourself to be a vessel of God's light will allow for more healing energy to enter within your own field. It's all connected with your own inner power and love—the miracle healings and knowing what is possible comes from within. The angels want you to feel empowered yourself, and they will help you do so. But I'm bringing this up because I don't want you to feel unworthy of this connection. You ARE worthy!

I don't know how everyone else feels in the angel community, but I feel like Archangel Raphael shows up with a team of angels. I feel like his energy is exciting, playful, compassionate, and incredibly understanding. He wants nothing more than to assist you with healing at a very high-frequency, miracle-making level. You have to trust in him and yourself. Feel into the changes and the health you really want. Start living like you are already healed. That frequency can truly change your life.

WRITING TO RAPHAEL

1. Archangel Raphael, please help heal any condition in my physical body that is blocking me from optimal health.

2. Archangel Raphael, show me the changes I need to make in my everyday patterns that will help me feel my absolute best.

3. Archangel Raphael, how can I improve my relationships? What needs to be cleared from my heart?

4. Archangel Raphael, do I have energy that is stuck and needs to flow? Help clear out any negativity or stuck energy from within.

CHAPTER 14
Archangel Jophiel

"Allow your heart to realize that your most profound transformation yet is the beauty that your light carries from within, without our human mind sabotaging our own recognition of oneself."
– Archangel Jophiel

I love this angel, and I absolutely love working with her! Archangel Jophiel is not as popular as the last three archangels, but it doesn't mean she is any less powerful, and she is full of love and healing. There are MANY archangels (more in my next book). They all have unique ways they can help each one of us who feels called to work with them.

Jophiel represents so much beauty, wisdom, joy, and truth. I see her a lot around females who are really seeking self-love from within. Her energy is light but powerful at the same time; she has very feminine energy and is a beautiful and joyful angel.

I feel like self-care is an overused word these days, and it can mean so many things for so many people. So many of us feel guilty when we take the time for self-care, which really is just a word for taking care of yourself, appreciating yourself, and really valuing and investing in *you*! Whatever your self-care is, Jophiel is the angel who wants to remind you that you are *worthy* of it. You are allowed to feel good and take care of yourself. Like I said, this can look completely different for all of us, but it is important. It shows up in your heart when you feel good about yourself.

Jophiel is also a truth seeker. She likes to help people when they are searching for a deeper truth from within. She wants everyone to know that trusting yourself and loving yourself is a form of self-care. This is so important these days because there is so much different information thrown at us. She likes to remind us that when we are connected to our own truth, it's easier for us to feel the truth outside of us as well.

She is an energy that, to me, is pink and yellow. Yellow really represents self-confidence and your own power. She is bold, energetic, endearing, and beautiful. She loves to help brighten your spirit, assist you with any goals you are currently seeking, and really help transform you and your light from the inside out. No wonder I feel so connected to this angel!

We become so busy in today's world that we forget how the little steps of taking care of ourselves have deep and powerful meaning and affect our everyday lives. It helps us sleep better, feel better, lift our moods and our spirits. So, I feel like she is really encouraging all of us to let go of any shame and guilt that comes from dedicating time to the things that make us feel good from the inside out. Or the outside in!

Her energy is playful and curious to me, and she has extraordinary love/friendship vibes. I love teaching other women about her, but she assists with masculine energy, too. I feel like she helps men connect to more of their hearts. She assists them with really engaging with themselves on a deeper level and allowing their own masculine energy and feminine energy to combine with their most powerful self and truth. They need to know their vulnerable parts. They need to have the space to feel soft and let go at times. And this also helps them find their truth and really engage with parts of themselves that have been closed off for so long.

Jophiel also loves to remind us about being a friend to ourselves as well. Taking the time to nurture our spirit and our mind has a profound effect on us as a whole. When we feel good about ourselves, we engage differently with others. We can forget about this part of us so easily. We, like so many other things, disconnect from our deepest desires to feel good. We engage through our day-to-day lives and run around endlessly and tirelessly. This becomes like we are running on low fuel. Even though we may be getting things done or pouring into others, how do we feel deep within? I feel like she is saying, "What is it that you need to do right now that will provide extra nurturing quality for your spirit?" Don't ignore this part of you; embrace it. She is saying to stop making excuses. It's time to also pour into yourself. You have so much love from within; it's time to shine.

What does this mean for you? Nurturing foods for your body? More joyful experiences? More movement? More sunshine? Laughing more? There are numerous ways to help ourselves. It's time you truly allow this for yourself because it will magnify everyone's spirits around you.

She is also reminding you to be playful! Have fun and experience life. We all get so stuck in the heaviness of our day to day, we forget to laugh. Play. Enjoy our time here. What is it that you need to go and do that will bring you more joy?

So, add Jophiel to your list of angels to start connecting with. As I have said many times before, they can be life-changing. We have to remember that they are not physical beings. They are energy, just like God. We have to have faith in them. Trust that they are here to help us and assist humanity when we ask for their help. They are incredible beings of light!

WRITING TO JOPHIEL

1. Archangel Jophiel, I would love you to help and assist me with understanding my own truth. I want to remember who I really am. What is something that will help me with this?

_____
_____
_____
_____

2. Archangel Jophiel, I need to practice more self-love and not feel so guilty about it when I do. Please help free my mind from any shame or guilt if I take some time for myself today.

3. Archangel Jophiel, what is something that I need to work on to be able to connect with my own heart on a deeper level? How can I return to my Joy?

Conclusion

"Truth really helps enlighten our souls' memory. It's the starting of a deep transformation from within. Powerful yet filled with love and compassion not only for ourselves but for humanity as a whole. Know and understand that you are capable of leading yourself into any achievement your heart desires. Do not limit your soul. Allow yourself to truly live, remembering where you came from and how to use this part of you to bring up the most magical-filled years to come. It's the beginning of a new time. Start to truly embrace the authenticity of your own wisdom. Each one of you carries a unique light code. It's powerful beyond measure. Don't use your wisdom to control, manipulate, or confuse others. Instead, embrace your beauty, love, wisdom, compassion, and set yourself free."
– The Angels

If nothing else, I hope this book inspires you to show up authentically as YOU. I hope it sparks curiosity and joy in your own heart. I really want people to understand that the world needs more heart. More truth. We need the authenticity! I hope sharing my own unique story also helps you on your own wellness path to feel whole. At times when we feel like we've tried everything, maybe it's time to really turn inward and look for the answers within us instead of outside of us.

The world needs more faith, but not the kind that is angry or controlling. We need the kind that is inside your own heart, and it's been there a long time, begging to come alive. I am deeply passionate that this is the missing puzzle piece for so many of us. In a world filled with disconnect, we need nothing more than to feel connected to this part of us. It is truly "spiritual wellness," the part of wellness that I talk about a lot these days.

Angels are nothing short of amazing and I love hearing other people's angel stories or "experiences" they can't quite explain or even believe in themselves. They just know there is something that is bigger than them, and they trust it. There are a lot of people who have experienced angels in different ways and have stories of their own. Keep sharing your stories! There really is magic in our everyday life. We just have to be open to experiencing it!

I hope you guys can take in any information that resonated with you and understand how absolutely amazing and powerful you really are, how worthy you are, how much purpose you have here, and that you are really needed. The most important thing to know and always remember is that you are not alone. It's easy to forget all these things if we only listen to the outside noise. It's really time to come back to yourself and God. Learn, grow, heal, and expand! Live the life you have always known you are capable of living. Or maybe live the life you never believed in in the first place! There are endless opportunities, love, and abundance for all of us that are here. We don't have to be wrapped up in our hurt, our anxiety, our jealousy, other people's voices, or our ego. Really take control of your own life and pursue the love from within that was always there to begin with.

Well, friends, as we come to the end of this book, I just really want to thank you. I prayed for you to be here reading this, and I prayed it would open people's minds and hearts to not only what I'm saying but to open your eyes to a path in front of you that is taking you deeper into who you really are. I am not here to prove anything I am saying is true. I can feel it with my entire heart. But I am also not here to prove or defend if I'm right or wrong. I am here sharing my own story and my own heart. This book took a lot of courage for me to write for many reasons. It also took me on my own deeper healing path and into much of what I didn't even know was buried within me. The words just flew out and let me really share what I have come to know over the past few years. I hope you can feel my heart throughout this book and that it inspires you to turn around and expand your own. I am sending a tremendous amount of love to each one of you. I believe in YOU.

Thank you. You are loved. You are worthy. You have purpose!

Thank You for Reading my Book!

DOWNLOAD YOUR FREE GIFT!

Connect to the most authentic version of yourself: A guide to connecting with the Archangels, no strings attached!

Scan the QR Code to Download:

I appreciate your interest in my book and value your feedback as it helps me improve future versions of this book. I would appreciate it if you could leave your invaluable review on Amazon.com with your feedback. Thank you!

www.ingramcontent.com/pod-product-compliance
Lightning Source LLC
LaVergne TN
LVHW041338080426
835512LV00006B/513